THE ULTIMATE UNOFFICIAL WORLD CUP BOOK

HarperCollins Children's Books, a division of HarperCollins Publishers,
195 Broadway, New York, NY 10007

HarperCollins Publishers, Macken House,
39/40 Mayor Street Upper, Dublin 1, D01 C9W8, Ireland

HarperPop is an imprint of HarperCollins Publishers.

The Ultimate Unofficial World Cup Book: Legends, Stats, and Stories from Soccer's Biggest Game

harpercollins.com

Library of Congress Control Number: 2025945449

ISBN 978-0-06-346840-5

Typography by Georgia Rucker

25 26 27 28 29 PCA 10 9 8 7 6 5 4 3 2 1

First Edition

THE ULTIMATE UNOFFICIAL WORLD CUP BOOK

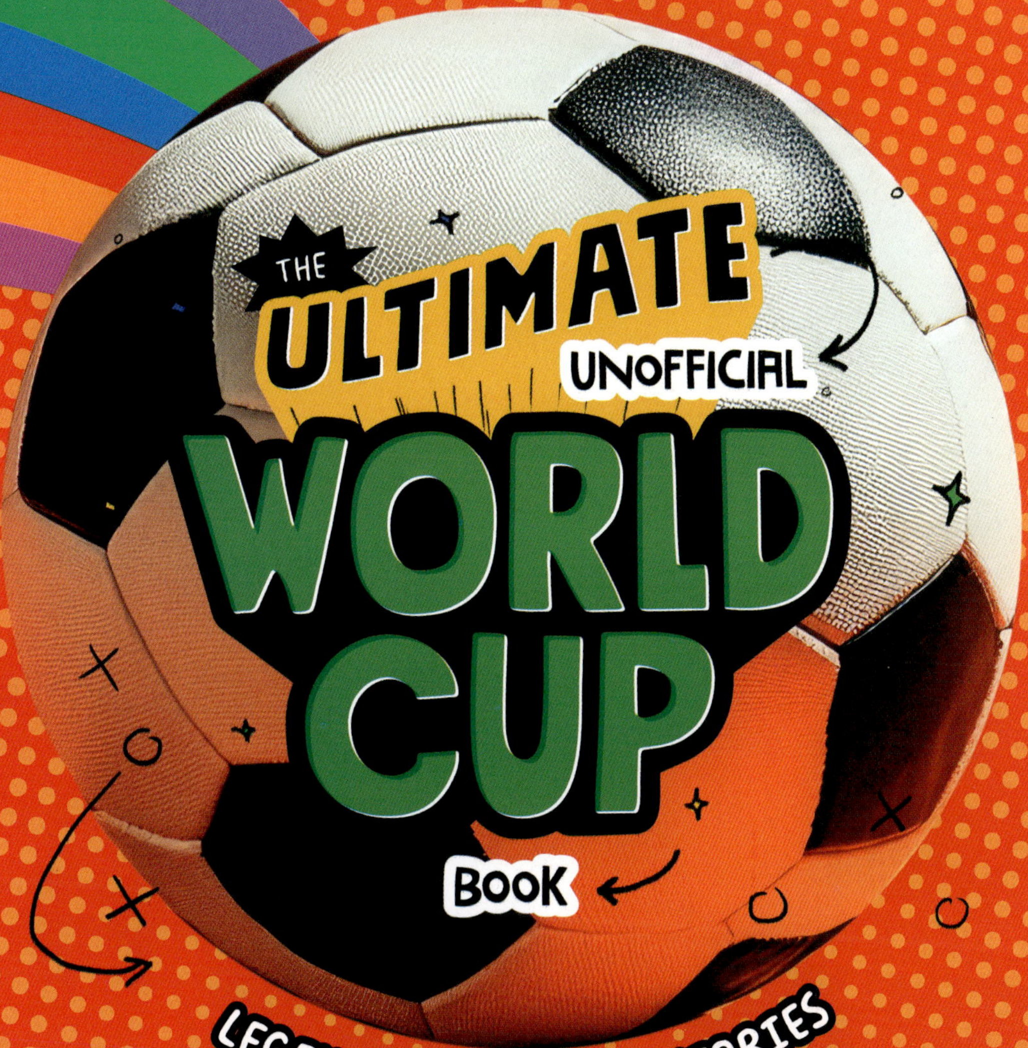

LEGENDS, STATS, AND STORIES FROM SOCCER'S BIGGEST GAME

BY MARIA S. BARBO

HARPER POP
An Imprint of HarperCollinsPublishers

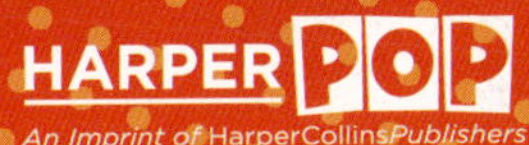

Contents

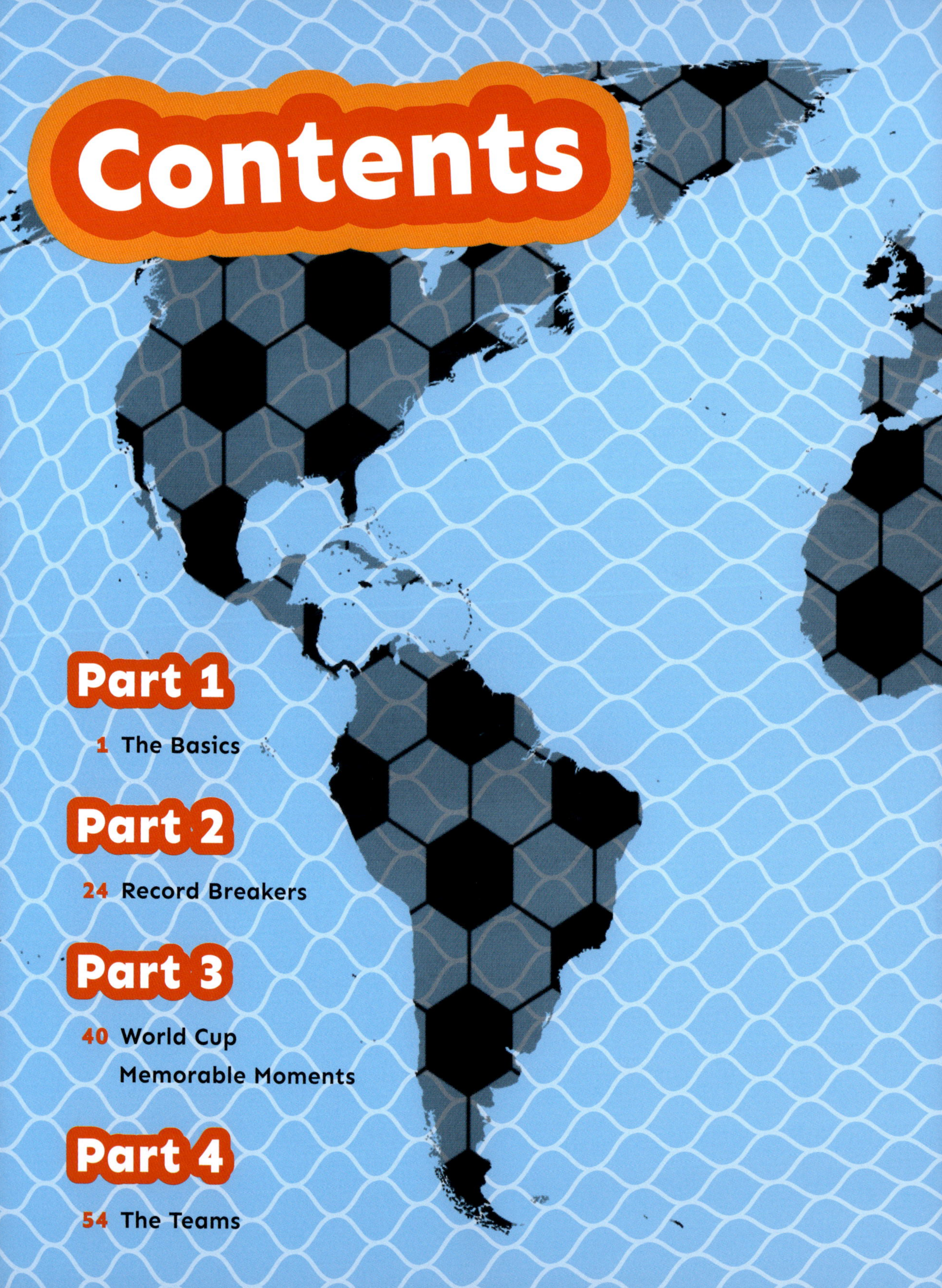

Part 1

Part 2

Part 3

Part 4

PART 1: THE BASICS

What Is the World Cup?

The World Cup is *the* biggest international soccer tournament. Period. Full stop.

Once every four years, countries from across the globe—representing North America, South America, Central America, the Caribbean, Europe, Africa, Asia, and the Pacific Islands—come together to compete for the glory of being the best in the world.

North America

South America

Europe

Central America

Pacific Islands

Africa

Asia

the Caribbean

The World Cup is hands down *the* most watched sporting event in the world—more popular than the Super Bowl, the World Series, the NBA finals, the tennis Grand Slams—and even the Olympics.

And in 2026, it takes place in the USA, Mexico, and Canada.

World Cup Firsts for 2026

3 HOST COUNTRIES
instead of 1!

CANADA

Canada will host for the very first time!

USA

The USA will play their first World Cup with brand-new head coach Mauricio Pochettino.

MEXICO

Mexico will be the first country to play host *three* times!

48
COUNTRIES
instead of 32!
104
MATCHES
instead of 64!
A BRAND-NEW
KNOCKOUT
STAGE
—the round of 32!
A GUARANTEED
SPOT FOR ONE
TEAM FROM
THE OCEANIA
CONFEDERATION.
Hello, New Zealand!
FAMOUS FIRST!
In 2022, French referee, Stéphanie Frappart became the first woman to officiate at a men's World Cup match!
TIME OUT
FOR TRIVIA!
Where was the very first World Cup played?
Answer: Estadio Centenario in Montevideo, Uruguay, in 1930!

The WHEN and WHERE of World Cup 2026

For **39** days between **June 11, 2026,** and **July 19, 2026, 48** teams from **48** countries will play **104** matches in **16** cities across **3** host countries—the US, Mexico, and Canada—as they compete for **1** trophy in the **23rd** World Cup.

VANCOUVER

SEATTLE

SAN FRANCISCO BAY AREA

LOS ANGELES

MONTERREY

GUADALAJARA

Where will *you* watch?

CANADA
TORONTO
BOSTON
KANSAS CITY
PHILADELPHIA
NEW JERSEY/NEW YORK
LAST STOP: THE FINAL!
1
• Sunday, July 19, 2026
• MetLife Stadium
• East Rutherford, New Jersey
• Holds 82,500 fans
ATLANTA
DALLAS
HOUSTON
MEXICO CITY
GAME #1
• Sunday, June 11, 2026
• Estadio Azteca
• Mexico City
• Holds 87,523 fans
MIAMI

The *WHEN* and *WHERE* of World Cup 2026

This tri-nation hosting aims to bring the World Cup closer to fans across North America, showcasing a diverse range of cultures and stadiums and setting the stage for the most expansive World Cup in history.

FUN FACT! The legendary Estadio Azteca hosted the opening games and World Cup finals in 1970 and 1986!

FUN FACT! Mexico will play all three of their group games on home turf.

RECORD BREAKER

Estadio Azteca will become the first stadium to host *three* World Cup group stage matches.

FUN FACT! Canada will play their opening match at BMO Field in Toronto, which was built as a soccer-specific stadium in 2007!

Tournament Timeline

Here's the need-to-know info on who plays who and when.

GROUP STAGE

June 11, 2026, to June 27, 2026

48 teams are broken into 12 groups of 4 teams each.

- Each team plays every other team in their group once.
- Games can end in a tie.
- The top 2 teams in each group—and the 8 best third-place teams—move on to the Round of 32.

FUN FACT! A random draw decides which teams play in which group!

ROUND OF 32

June 28, 2026, to July 3, 2026

A WORLD CUP FIRST!

- The group winners play the runners-up from different groups.
- Knockout round games cannot end in a tie. If a team loses a game, they go home!

ROUND OF 16

July 4, 2026, to July 7, 2026

- Same as the Round of 32 but with 16 teams this time!
- Eight winning teams move on to the Quarterfinals.

KNOCKOUT ROUND

QUARTERFINALS

July 9, 2026, to July 11, 2026

- Eight teams play a total of four games.
- Teams that have already played each other in the Round of 16 won't play each other again.
- Four winning teams move on to the Semifinals

KNOCKOUT ROUND

SEMIFINALS

July 14, 2025, to July 15, 2026

- Only four teams left!
- There are two games in this round.
- The winners go to the finals!

THE FINAL

July 19, 2026

- Winner takes all!

KNOCKOUT ROUND

THIRD-PLACE PLAYOFF

July 18, 2026

- The two teams that didn't win in the Semifinals play to see who comes in third!

On the Clock

GAME TIME

All soccer games are 90 minutes long plus stoppage time. That's two 45-minute halves with a 15-minute break in between.

STOPPAGE TIME

The clock keeps running in soccer—even when play stops. So the time it takes to deal with a foul, injury, or substitution gets added up and tacked on to the end of each half.

No Sudden Death! Unlike in some other sports, the game doesn't stop as soon as someone scores a goal. All 20 minutes of extra time are played—no matter what!

TIME OUT FOR TRIVIA!

The average stoppage time is one to five minutes. Which World Cup tournament had the most stoppage time ever?

Answer: 2022 in Qatar. An average of 11.61 minutes was added to each game.

EXTRA TIME

Lots of soccer games end in a tie—and that's A-OK! But when there *has* to be a winner—like in the knockout and final rounds of the World Cup—two extra 15-minute halves are played.

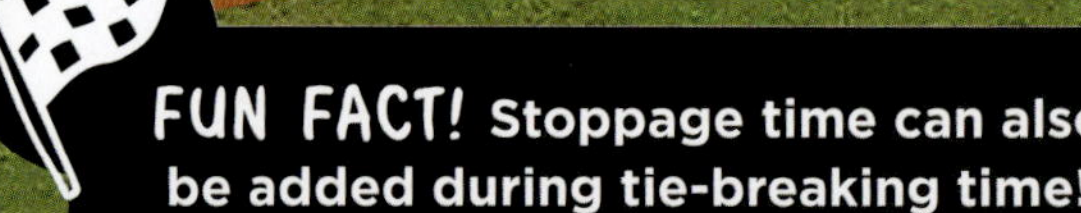

FUN FACT! Stoppage time can also be added during tie-breaking time!

PENALTY SHOOT-OUT

The ultimate soccer tiebreaker. When a game is still tied after extra time, five different players from each team get to kick the ball toward the goal from 12 yards in front of it. As soon as one team has a lead that the other team can't match, they win!

TAKE NOTE: Only players who are *on the field* when the game ends can take part in the penalty shoot-out.

Luck of the draw! A coin toss decides which team takes the first kick!

ONLY THREE WORLD CUP FINALS ENDED IN A PENALTY SHOOT-OUT!

TIME OUT FOR TRIVIA!

Do you know how many World Cups ended after extra time?

Answer: Five.

World Cup Winners

There have been 22 World Cup tournaments total. Who made it to the finals? Who won? What was the score? And who vied for third and fourth place? This map shows it all!

TIME OUT FOR TRIVIA!

There were no World Cup tournaments in 1942 or 1946. Do you know why? Take a guess!

Answer: Because of World War II!

1994 UNITED STATES

WINNER Brazil v Italy (3–2)
Sweden v Bulgaria (4–0)

1966 ENGLAND

WINNER England v Germany (4–2)
Portugal v Soviet Union (2–1)

1982 SPAIN

WINNER Italy v West Germany (3–1)
Poland v France (3–2)

1970 MEXICO

WINNER Brazil v Italy (4–1)
West Germany v Uruguay (1–0)

1986 MEXICO

WINNER Argentina v West Germany (3–2)
France v Belgium (4–2)

1950 BRAZIL

WINNER Uruguay v Brazil (2–1)
Sweden v Spain (3–1)

2014 BRAZIL

WINNER Germany v Argentina (1–0)
Netherlands v Brazil (3–0)

1962 CHILE

WINNER Brazil v Czechoslovakia (3–1)
Chile v Yugoslavia (1–0)

1978 ARGENTINA

WINNER Argentina v Netherlands (3–1)
Brazil v Italy (2–1)

1930 URUGUAY

WINNER Uruguay v Argentina (4–2)
United States v Yugoslavia (there was no third-place match)

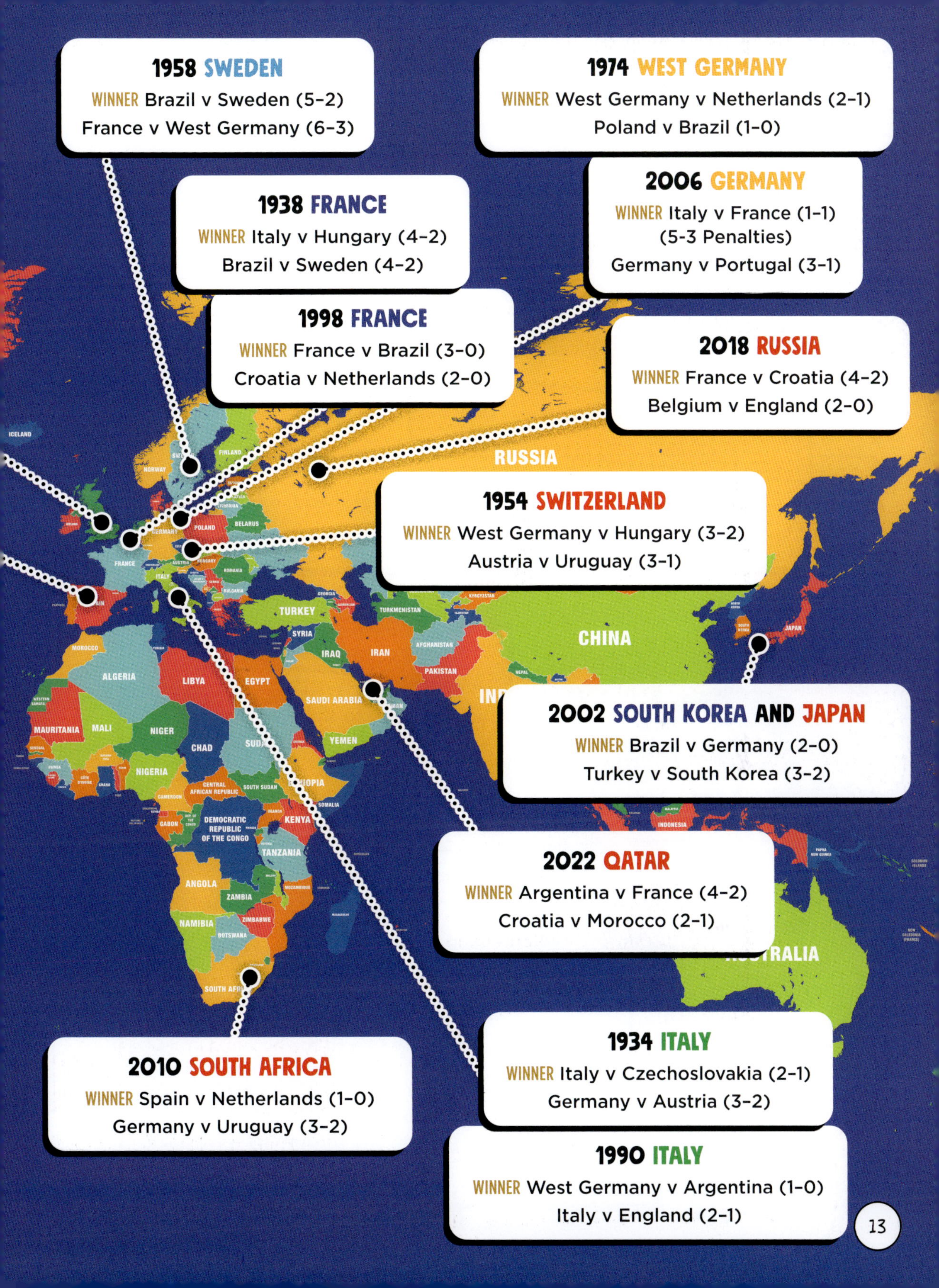

1958 SWEDEN

WINNER Brazil v Sweden (5-2)
France v West Germany (6-3)

1974 WEST GERMANY

WINNER West Germany v Netherlands (2-1)
Poland v Brazil (1-0)

1938 FRANCE

WINNER Italy v Hungary (4-2)
Brazil v Sweden (4-2)

2006 GERMANY

WINNER Italy v France (1-1)
(5-3 Penalties)
Germany v Portugal (3-1)

1998 FRANCE

WINNER France v Brazil (3-0)
Croatia v Netherlands (2-0)

2018 RUSSIA

WINNER France v Croatia (4-2)
Belgium v England (2-0)

1954 SWITZERLAND

WINNER West Germany v Hungary (3-2)
Austria v Uruguay (3-1)

2002 SOUTH KOREA AND JAPAN

WINNER Brazil v Germany (2-0)
Turkey v South Korea (3-2)

2022 QATAR

WINNER Argentina v France (4-2)
Croatia v Morocco (2-1)

2010 SOUTH AFRICA

WINNER Spain v Netherlands (1-0)
Germany v Uruguay (3-2)

1934 ITALY

WINNER Italy v Czechoslovakia (2-1)
Germany v Austria (3-2)

1990 ITALY

WINNER West Germany v Argentina (1-0)
Italy v England (2-1)

Soccer Rules and Regulations

What do you need to know to enjoy the World Cup? Check this out!

THE OBJECTIVE

Two teams with 11 players each—including one goalie—score by getting the ball in the other team's goal.

RULE #1 THE KEY PRINCIPLE

Hands off! Players can move the ball with their feet, head, and chest but not arms or hands—unless they're the goalie!

MAKE A MOVE!

HEADER: Using your head to shoot or pass the ball. Does that sometimes cause headbutts and concussions? It sure does!

HAND BALL: The foul that's called when someone other than the goalie uses their hand, elbow, arm, or shoulder to move the ball.

TACKLE: Using your feet to take the ball away from an opponent.

SLIDE TACKLE: Sliding on the ground to win the ball. WARNING! Could cause injuries and fouls!

THROW-IN: The exception to the no-hands rule. When the ball goes out anywhere, a player from the other team throws it back in using a two-handed, overhead throw. They have to keep both feet on the ground and throw from behind the sideline.

Lionel Messi of **Argentina** heads the ball against **Netherlands** during the 2022 World Cup.

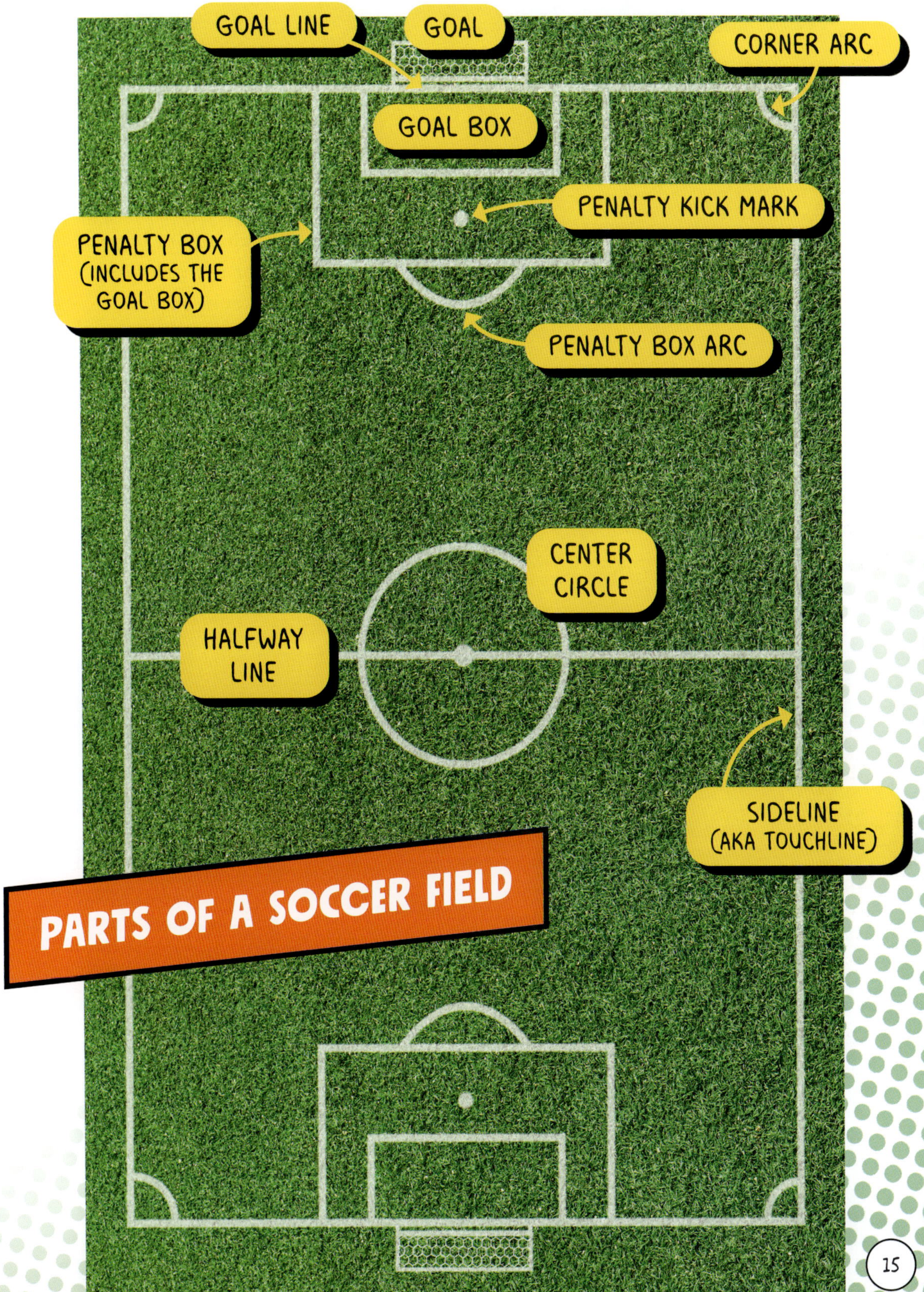
GOAL LINE
GOAL
CORNER ARC
GOAL BOX
PENALTY KICK MARK
PENALTY BOX (INCLUDES THE GOAL BOX)
PENALTY BOX ARC
CENTER CIRCLE
HALFWAY LINE
SIDELINE (AKA TOUCHLINE)
PARTS OF A SOCCER FIELD

All Kinds of Kicks

CORNER KICK

Happens inside the corner arc. If a defender is the last person to touch the ball before it goes out of play *over the goal line*, the attacking team gets to kick the ball back in from the corner arc.

Neymar of **Brazil** takes a corner kick during the 2018 group stage match.

FUN FACT! Teams *love* corner kicks because they get to set up plays—called **set pieces**—and try to score a goal.

GOAL KICK

If an attacker is the last person to touch the ball before it goes out of bounds *over the goal line*, the goalie gets to kick the ball back onto the field. The other team stays *outside* the penalty box and penalty arc until the ball is kicked.

PENALTY KICK

When a serious foul is called *inside the goal box*—for things like kicking, tripping, charging, or pushing—the other team gets to kick the ball directly toward the goal from the penalty mark.

Randal Kolo Muani scores France's fourth penalty in a penalty shoot out during the 2022 World Cup between **Argentina** and **France**.

FREE KICKS

FREE KICK: The punishment for offsides (more on this later), fouls, and things goalies aren't supposed to do inside the penalty box—like take more than four steps while controlling the ball. The other team gets to kick the ball from the spot where the foul happened.

DIRECT FREE KICKS: When the foul is so serious it could have caused an injury, the kicker can aim straight for the goal.

INDIRECT FREE KICKS: For less serious fouls, like blocking an opponent, the kicker has to pass the ball to another player before he can score.

FUN FACT! Some players, like French GOAT Zinedine Zidane, are known for their skill at free kicks and penalty kicks!

Top 5 Most Shocking World Cup Moments

From headbutts to biting to spitting—*yikes!*—here are some of the most *stunning* moments in World Cup history.

1. ZIDANE'S HEADBUTT, 2006

Italian defender Marco Materazzi mouths off to French midfielder Zinedine Zidane during extra time in the 2006 World Cup finals—so Zidane headbutts him right in the chest! Zidane gets kicked out of the game and France loses to Italy in the penalty shoot-out.

2. "THE HAND OF GOD," 1986

Infamous Argentine superstar Diego Maradona gets away with the hand ball of all hand balls when he *punches* the ball into the goal during the 1986 quarterfinal match against England. He later claims the "hand of God" scored the goal.

3. SUAREZ BITES, 2014

Star Uruguayan striker Luis Suarez leaves his mark on the 2014 group stage when he reportedly bites Italian defender Giorgio Chiellini. No foul is called but Suarez later gets banned from all soccer activities for four months and must pay a $100,000 fine.

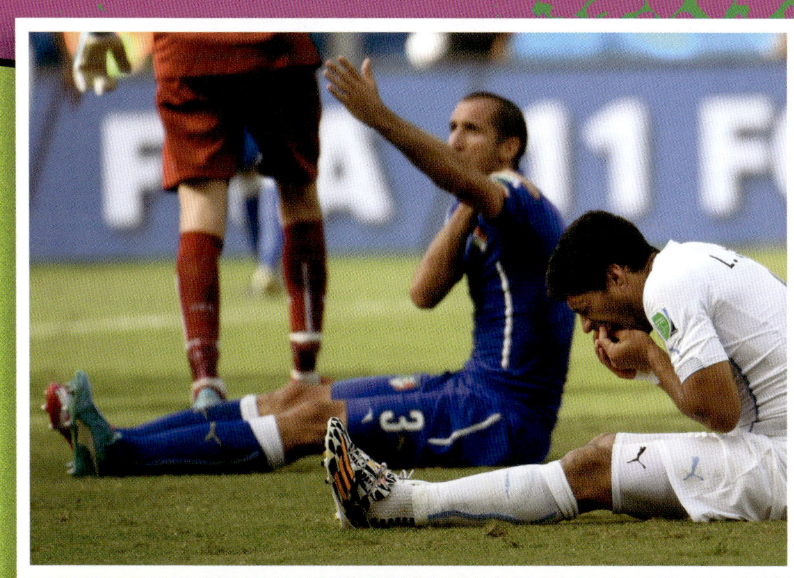

FUN FACT!

Breakfast of *chomp*-ians! This was the *third* time Suarez reportedly sank his teeth into another player.

4. RIJKAARD'S FOUL MOOD, 1990

Dutch midfielder Frank Rijkaard spits on German forward Rudi Völler *twice* during their round-of-sixteen match, earning himself a red card and the nickname "Llama."

5. SUAREZ'S HAND BALL, 2010

Uruguayan striker Luis Suarez shuts down Ghana's chance to become the first African nation to make it to the semifinals. How? By blocking Dominic Adiyah's header with his hand! He later celebrates when Asamoah Gyan's penalty kick bounces off the crossbar!

The Good, The Bad, and the Megged!

Some soccer moves go beyond the basics—and sometimes make headlines!

THE GOOD:

HAT TRICK: When a player scores *three* goals in *one* game.

BRACE: When one player scores two goals in the same match.

ASSIST: When a player makes a pass that directly leads to a goal.

FUN FACT! The "King of Football," Pelé, became the youngest player ever to score a hat trick in Brazil's 1958 semifinal game against France. And his record still stands!

THE BAD:

YELLOW CARD: A warning the referee gives for bad behavior or multiple fouls. He literally holds up a yellow card and points to the player at fault.

RED CARD: When a player gets two yellow cards in a World Cup match—or does something *truly awful* like head-butting another player—they're kicked out of the game and have to sit out the next game. Sometimes the foul is *so bad* they miss up to *three* games!

David Beckham's embarrassing red card incident

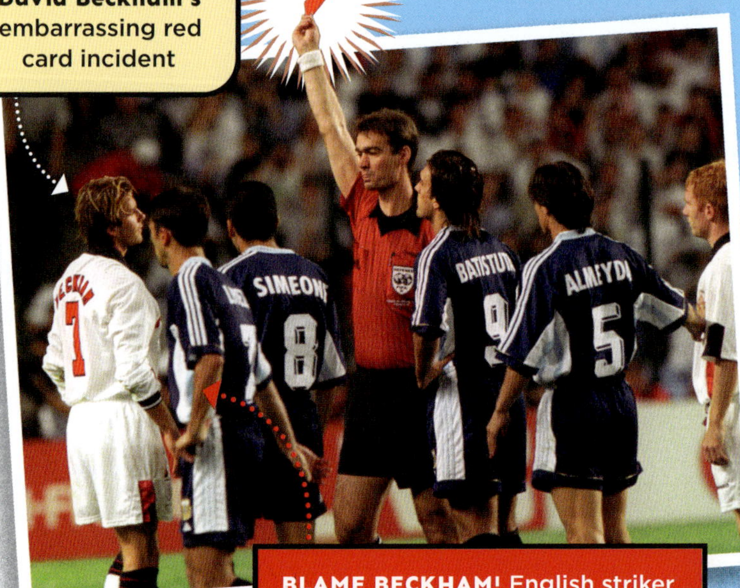

BLAME BECKHAM! English striker David Beckham gets kicked out of the 1998 Round-of-16 game against Argentina for *kicking* an opponent. He's not allowed to join the penalty shoot-out even though he's one of England's *best* kickers! England loses and gets sent home! And fans *still* blame Beckham!

FUN FACT! The 2006 World Cup saw the most red cards ever: 28 players sent off in only 20 matches!

THE MEGGED:

A **MEG** or **NUTMEG** is when a player passes the ball to himself by dribbling it through another player's legs. It's a great way to beat a defender and break away to score!

GOATS like Lionel Messi are great at it! But *getting* "megged"? That's just embarrassing.

FUN FACT!
Refs started using VAR—Video Assistant Referee—technology during the 2018 World Cup in Russia!

WHAT CONFUSES PEOPLE THE MOST ABOUT SOCCER?

THE OFFSIDE RULE

Where is the attacking player when the ball is played to him? If he's closer to the goal than the last defender, then he's *offside*. And any goal he scores *does not count*.

Bummer, right? Kind of. But it makes for a better game. The offside rule prevents **cherry picking**. That's when a player hangs out in front of the other team's goal to wait to get the ball and kick it in.

What was the most controversial offside call in World Cup history? In 2010, Argentina v Mexico in the Round of 16. Argentine striker Carlos Tevez's goal stands even though he's offside by a few yards. Argentina wins 3-1 and Mexico goes home!

FUN FACT!
Uruguay's José Batista got the quickest red card in World Cup history—*in the first 56 seconds* of a game against Scotland in 1986.

Trophies and Awards!

The top three teams take home a World Cup trophy—but those aren't the only awards earned at the tournament. Top players and teams get recognized for things like fair play, most entertaining team, and outstanding player of the finals. Here's a rundown.

GOLDEN BALL AWARD

Outstanding player of the World Cup finals

2022: Lionel Messi, Argentina

2018: Luka Modric, Croatia

2014: Lionel Messi, Argentina

2010: Diego Forlán, Uruguay

2006: Zinedine Zidane, France

2002: Oliver Kahn, Germany

FUN FACT! Lionel Messi is the only player in history to win twice!

GOLDEN GLOVE AWARD

Best goalkeeper of the tournament

2022: Emilio Martinez, Argentina

2018: Thibault Courtois, Belgium

2014: Manuel Neuer, Germany

2010: Iker Castillas, Spain

2006: Gianluigi Buffon, Italy

2002: Oliver Kahn, Germany

Trophy Troubles! The original Jules Rimet Trophy, which is given to the World Cup winner, was stolen *twice*—in 1966 and 1983. The first time, it was found under a bush by a dog named Pickles, but in 1983 it vanished for good—most likely melted down into gold bars!

GOLDEN BOOT AWARD

Highest scorer of the tournament

2022: Kylian Mbappé, France, 8

2018: Harry Kane, England, 7

2014: James Rodríguez, Colombia, 6

2010: Thomas Müller, Germany, 5

2006: Miroslav Klose, Germany, 5

2002: Ronaldo, Brazil, 8

In 2022, Lionel Messi came in second with seven goals!

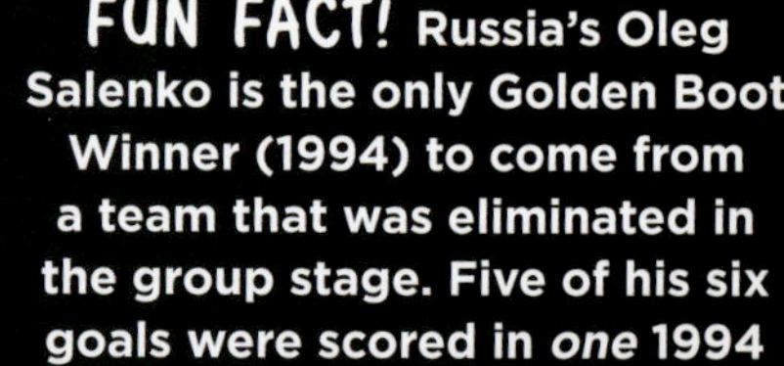

BEST YOUNG PLAYERS OF THE TOURNAMENT

2022: Enzo Fernandez, Argentina, 21

2018: Kylian Mbappé, France, 19

2014: Paul Pogba, France, 21

2010: Thomas Müller, Germany, 20

2006: Lukas Podolski, Germany, 21

2002: Landon Donovan, USA, 20

Landon Donovan made three World Cup appearances for the US National Team, in 2002, 2006, and 2010

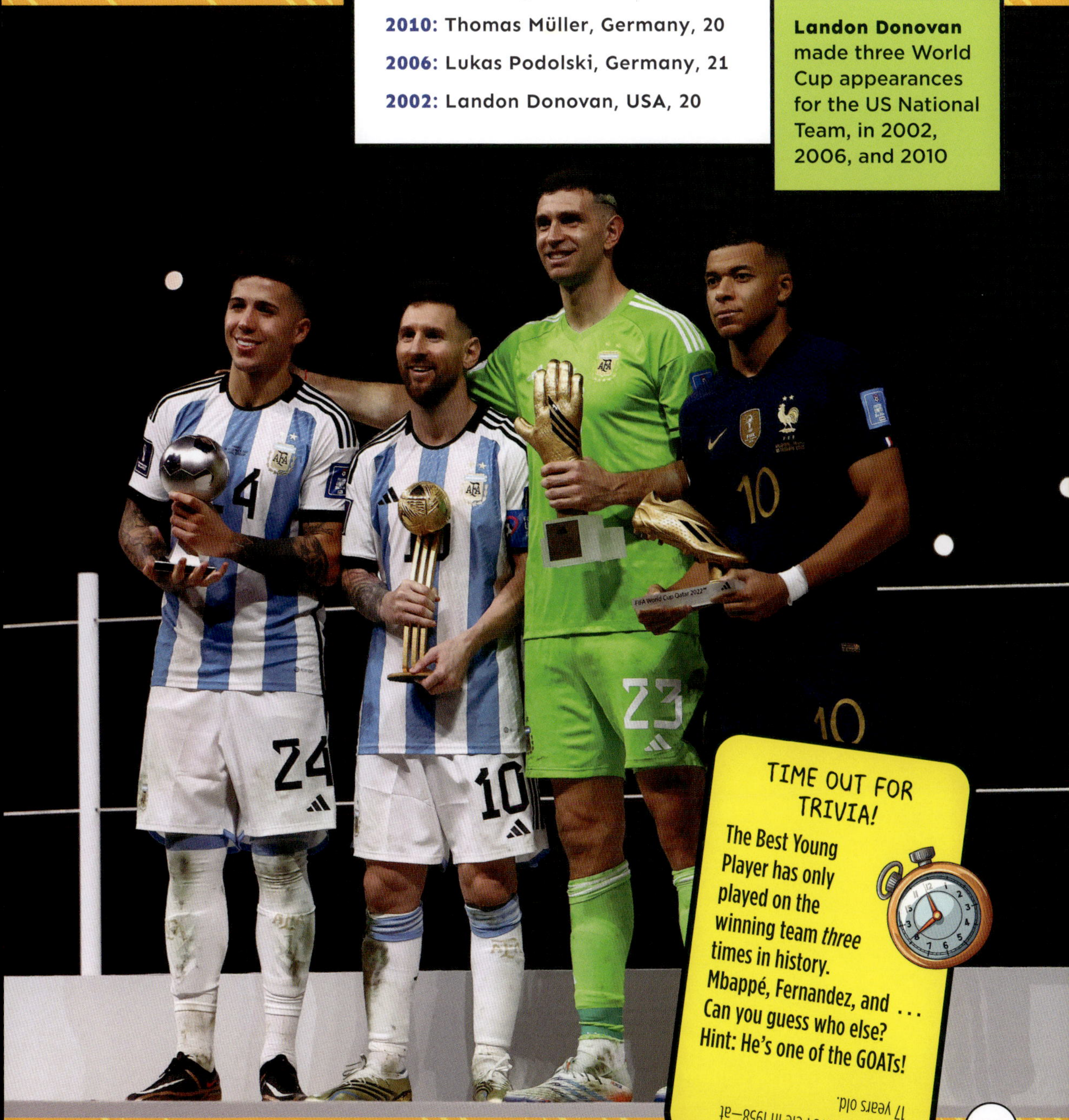

TIME OUT FOR TRIVIA!

The Best Young Player has only played on the winning team *three* times in history. Mbappé, Fernandez, and . . . Can you guess who else? Hint: He's one of the GOATs!

Answer: Brazil's Pelé in 1958—at 17 years old.

PART 2: RECORD-BREAKERS!

18

MOST YELLOW CARDS EVER AWARDED IN A WORLD CUP GAME

2022 quarterfinals, **Argentina** v **Netherlands**

FUN FACT! Two of them went to the same player—Dutch defender Denzel Dumfries—during the penalty shoot-out!

117 minutes

THE LONGEST GROUP STAGE GAME IN HISTORY

—and that's without extra time!

4

MOST RED CARDS EVER ISSUED IN A WORLD CUP GAME

2006 Round of 16, **Portugal** v **Netherlands**

FUN FACT! This game was so brutal, it was nicknamed "The Battle of Nuremberg!" Sixteen yellow cards were also given out!

5

MOST PENALTY KICKS AWARDED TO ONE TEAM IN A SINGLE WORLD CUP TOURNAMENT

(excluding shoot-outs)

2022, **Argentina**

20

MOST OFFSIDE CALLS IN A SINGLE GAME

England in 1982 Group Stage, England v Kuwait

5

MOST WORLD CUP WINS BY A SINGLE TEAM

Brazil in 1958, 1962, 1970, 1994, and 2002

8
THE MOST HAT TRICKS SCORED IN A SINGLE TOURNAMENT
1954, **Switzerland**

88
MOST INJURIES IN A WORLD CUP TOURNAMENT
2022, Qatar

2
MOST HAT TRICKS SCORED BY A SINGLE PLAYER IN A WORLD CUP TOURNAMENT
1954, **Sándor Kocsis, Hungary**

FUN FACT! The only tournament with no hat tricks scored at all was 2006 in Germany!

27 years, 267 days
YOUNGEST COACH OF A WORLD CUP–WINNING TEAM
Juan José Tramutola, Argentina, 1930

27 minutes
MOST STOPPAGE TIME ADDED TO A WORLD CUP GAME EVER
2022 Group Stage, **England v Iran**

Iranian goalkeeper Alireza Beiranvand violently collides with teammate **Majid Hosseini** at the beginning of the game, adding fourteen minutes—the most stoppage time ever added to a half!

45 Years, 161 days
OLDEST PLAYER IN A WORLD CUP GAME
Essam El-Hadary, Egypt, 2018

17 years, 41 Days
YOUNGEST PLAYER IN A WORLD CUP GAME
Norman Whiteside, Northern Ireland, 1982

Who's Who? Soccer Jerseys by the Numbers

Jersey numbers help fans and officials know who's who on the field. But what does the number on each player's jersey say about them?

The players in the starting lineup use numbers
1–11

In the World Cup, each team *has* to use the numbers
1–23

The numbers show the player's position.

THE BREAKDOWN:

In the World Cup:

number 1 is always the goalkeeper

2–5 are defensive players—who protect the goal

6–8 are midfielders—who create plays in the middle or who can either drop back to help defend or push forward to attack

9–11 are forwards—who are looking to score

NOTEWORTHY NUMBERS!

LUCKY #7 is usually worn by an attacking winger who supports the main striker. **David Beckham** and **Cristiano Ronaldo** are famous #7s.

USMNT GOAT **Clint Dempsey,** who played as both a midfielder *and* a forward, wore **jersey #8.**

FUN FACT! Ronaldo's nickname is a combo of his initials and jersey number: CR7!

FUN FACT!
#13 is usually saved for the backup goalkeeper.

The #10 jersey is almost always worn by an **attacking midfielder**, who creates plays and supports the main striker. Argentina's Lionel Messi, England's Harry "the Hurricane" Kane, and Brazil's Pelé are three of the most famous #10s.

Pelé & Maradona

There have been many great soccer players over the years, but only two have been named the Greatest of the Century: Brazil's unmatched talent, Pelé, and Argentina's genius, Diego Maradona.

PELÉ, BRAZIL

(October 23, 1940–December 29, 2022)

FULL NAME: Edson Arantes do Nascimento

HOMETOWN: Três Corações, Brazil

POSITION: Forward

JERSEY #: 10

NICKNAME: O Rei (the king)

At seventeen years old, Brazilian soccer legend Pelé was the youngest player to ever win a World Cup. He scored a brace—two goals—in the 1958 final against Sweden, and Brazil declared him a national treasure! His speed, versatility, and thrilling goals made him the most famous soccer player of his time.

Pelé holds the records for most World Cup wins for a single player. He won with Brazil in 1958, 1962, *and* 1970!

He's the all-time leading goal scorer for Brazil with 77 goals in 92 games.

He holds the record for the most assists in World Cup history.

He's in the *Guinness Book of World Records* for averaging almost one goal for every game he ever played: 1,279 goals in 1,363 games!

FUN FACT! **Pelé's style of play earned soccer the nickname "The Beautiful Game!"**

(*October 30, 1960–November 25, 2020*)

HOMETOWN: Lanús, Buenos Aires, Argentina

POSITION: Midfielder

JERSEY #: 10

NICKNAME: El Pibe de Oro ("The Golden Boy")

Diego Maradona had a big personality that fans loved—but he could also be controversial. He's responsible for one of the most shocking fouls in soccer history—punching the ball into the net—as well as some of its most beautiful goals.

He scored 5 goals and made 5 assists in the 1986 World Cup.

Maradona was the captain of the 1986 Argentine World Cup team that won against West Germany.

Maradona was fouled a record-breaking 152 times in World Cup play. Lionel Messi comes in second with 75. His opponents knew they had to stop him!

He was named the South American player of the year twice.

After he retired from playing, Maradona managed club teams in Mexico and Argentina and famously—and dramatically—led Argentina to the World Cup finals in 2010.

Messi vs Ronaldo

The Biggest Rivalry in Soccer GOAT History!

Pelé and Maradona may be the players of the century, but they never shared a field. Living legends Lionel Messi and Cristiano Ronaldo are playing at the top of their game at the same moment in history! They've faced off thirty-six times—but *never* in a World Cup game. Will this be the year they challenge each other on the world stage?

SO HOW DO MESSI AND RONALDO STACK UP?

FUN FACT! The rivalry between Messi and Ronaldo started as a famous club rivalry—known as "el clásico"—between their Spanish teams, FC Barcelona and Real Madrid.

LIONEL MESSI, ARGENTINA

Messi is a dribbling dynamo, known for his technical skills, passing, play-making, and goal scoring.

BIRTHDAY: June 24, 1987

HOMETOWN: Rosario, Argentina

NICKNAMES: La Pulga (the flea), La Pulga Atómica (because he is small yet fast and mighty)

POSITION: Forward

JERSEY #: 10

CLUB TEAM: Inter Miami CF

WORLD CUPS: 2006, 2010, 2014, 2018, and 2022

FUN FACT! Maradona was Messi's coach 2008–2020.

- Messi is the only player to score in a World Cup in his teens, 20s, and 30s.
- Messi captained a record-breaking 19 World Cup matches.
- Messi won the 2022 World Cup with Argentina.
- Messi has scored 13 World Cup goals.
- Messi has made 8 World Cup assists.
- Messi holds the record for most goals in one calendar year: 91 in 2012.
- Messi holds the record for most minutes played by a single player in World Cup history: 2,314.

CRISTIANO RONALDO, PORTUGAL

Cristiano Ronaldo is a goal-scoring machine known for cutting in from the left wing and shooting with his powerful right foot.

BIRTHDAY: February 5, 1985

HOMETOWN: Fuchal, Portugal

NICKNAMES: CR7, "El Bicho" (the bug), "Penaldo" (because of so many successful penalty kicks)

POSITION: Forward

JERSEY #: 7

CLUB TEAM: Saudi Pro League club Al-Nassr

WORLD CUPS: 2006, 2010, 2014, 2018, and 2022

Ronaldo is the first and only male player to score in 5 different World Cup tournaments!

Ronaldo captained 11 World Cup matches.

Portugal hasn't won a World Cup—*yet*. Will this be the year?

Ronaldo has scored 8 World Cup goals.

Ronaldo has made 2 World Cup assists.

Ronaldo is the oldest player to ever score a hat trick in the World Cup: 2018 against Spain, 33 years old.

Ronaldo has scored the most international goals (136 for Portugal) and holds the record for most international appearances (219).

WHO DO YOU THINK WILL BE THE NEXT BIG SOCCER RIVALRY?

The GOATS

Who else measures up to Pelé and Maradona? Here are ten of the most influential soccer players in soccer history.

JOHAN CRUYFF, attacking midfielder and second striker for the Netherlands, was so talented he changed the game. He invented a dribbling skill during the 1974 World Cup finals called the "Cruyff Turn" *and* popularized a whole style of play called "Total Football!"

WHAT'S THE CRUYFF TURN? During the Netherlands 1974 group stage game against Sweden, Cruyff faked a pass, pulled the ball behind his standing leg, then changed directions. Now players all over the world learn this dribbling skill!

WHAT'S TOTAL FOOTBALL? A flexible attacking style where players switch roles to create plays—making it *really* hard for opponents to defend against them.

ZINEDINE ZIDANE, a midfielder for France is one of the best—and most elegant—playmakers of all time. A genius at free kicks, penalty kicks, and ball control, he played in three World Cups—1998, 2002, and 2006—and won in 1998!

RONALDO NAZÁRIO DE LIMA played in five World Cups for Brazil—2006, 2010, 2014, 2018, 2022—where he scored a total of eight *phenomenal* goals. He was one of the fastest and most powerful two-footed goal scorers and dribblers of all time, but knee injuries kept him from becoming number one!

Beckenbauer is one of just three players—along with Mário Zagallo and Didier Deschamps—who've won the World Cup as a player (in 1974) *and* as a manager (1990)!

Player, coach, manager, leader: Germany's **FRANZ BECKENBAUER** is one of the greatest all-around players ever. He was a central defender and *still* scored goals all the time. In fact, he created the role of sweeper! He played in the World Cup in 1966, 1970, and 1974.

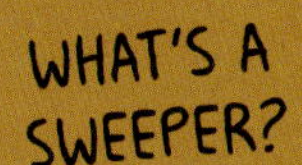

The sweeper clears any dangerous balls that get past the defensive line before they make it to the goalkeeper.

MICHEL PLATINI, "Le Roi" (The King), midfielder for France, was one of the best passers and free-kick specialists in soccer history and previously held the record for all-time top goal scorer for France. He played in three World Cups: 1978, 1982, and 1986.

Known for his slide tackles and two-footedness, **PAOLO MALDINI** of Italy is one of the greatest defenders in soccer history. He played in four World Cups (1990, 1994, 1998, and 2002) and against other greats like Maradona, Ronaldo, and Platini.

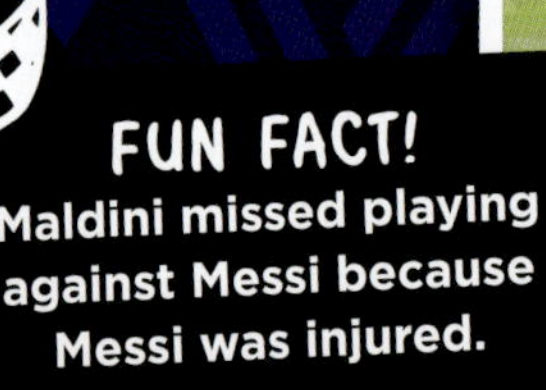

FUN FACT!
Maldini missed playing against Messi because Messi was injured.

Hungarian striker and 1954 team captain **FERENC PÚSKAS** scored so many technically brilliant and beautiful goals, the award for best men's goal of the year was named after him!

World Cup legend **GERD MÜLLER** of West Germany, aka "Der Bomber," scored ten goals in the 1970 tournament and four in the 1974 final against Italy—including the winning goal!

Brazil's **MANÉ GARRINCHA** is one of the best dribblers ever. He was the first player to win the Golden Ball, Golden Boot, and the World Cup final trophy in the same tournament!

One of Portugal's greatest, **EUSÉBIO DA SILVA FERREIRA**, scored a total of 733 goals in only 745 games during his career and helped his team win third place in the 1966 World Cup. His nickname was "the Black Panther" because of his speed and agility!

Who would make it onto YOUR top ten list?

Giuseppe Meazza, Franco Baresi, or Robert Baggio of Italy? Bobby Charlton of England, Andrés Iniesta of Spain, or a current rising star?

World Cups by the Numbers

The World Cup has a lot of teams—and there's a lot going on. How does it all add up?

10–25
average number of balls on hand per game for quicker restarts and play

FUN FACT! All balls are marked with the team, date, and location of the game so they can become souvenirs for teams, referees, host cities, or lucky fans!

8
number of national teams who've won the World Cup

80
number of nations who've played in at least one World Cup final

WORLD CUP WATCH PARTY!

3.4 million

number of people who attended the 2022 World Cup in Qatar

1.5 billion

number of people who tuned in for at least one minute of the 2022 final

FUN FACT! According to Nielsen, the 2024 Super Bowl drew only an average audience of 186.2 million viewers—123.7 million in the US and 62.5 million internationally.

6–7

average number of miles a soccer player runs during a 90-minute game—depending on position and team strategy. That's 9.7 to 11.3 kilometers!

Central midfielders run the most! French midfielder **N'Golo Kanté** runs an average of 7.5–8 miles per game.

HOW DOES THAT STACK UP AGAINST...?

1.25 average miles run per American football game	0.046 (about 242 feet) average miles run per baseball game	2.5 to 3.1 average miles run per a 48-minute basketball game

Right on the Money!

Hosting the World Cup can be pricey. There are the costs of building or fixing up stadiums, roads, and transportation—along with the costs of security, event managing, power supply, marketing, wages, and more!

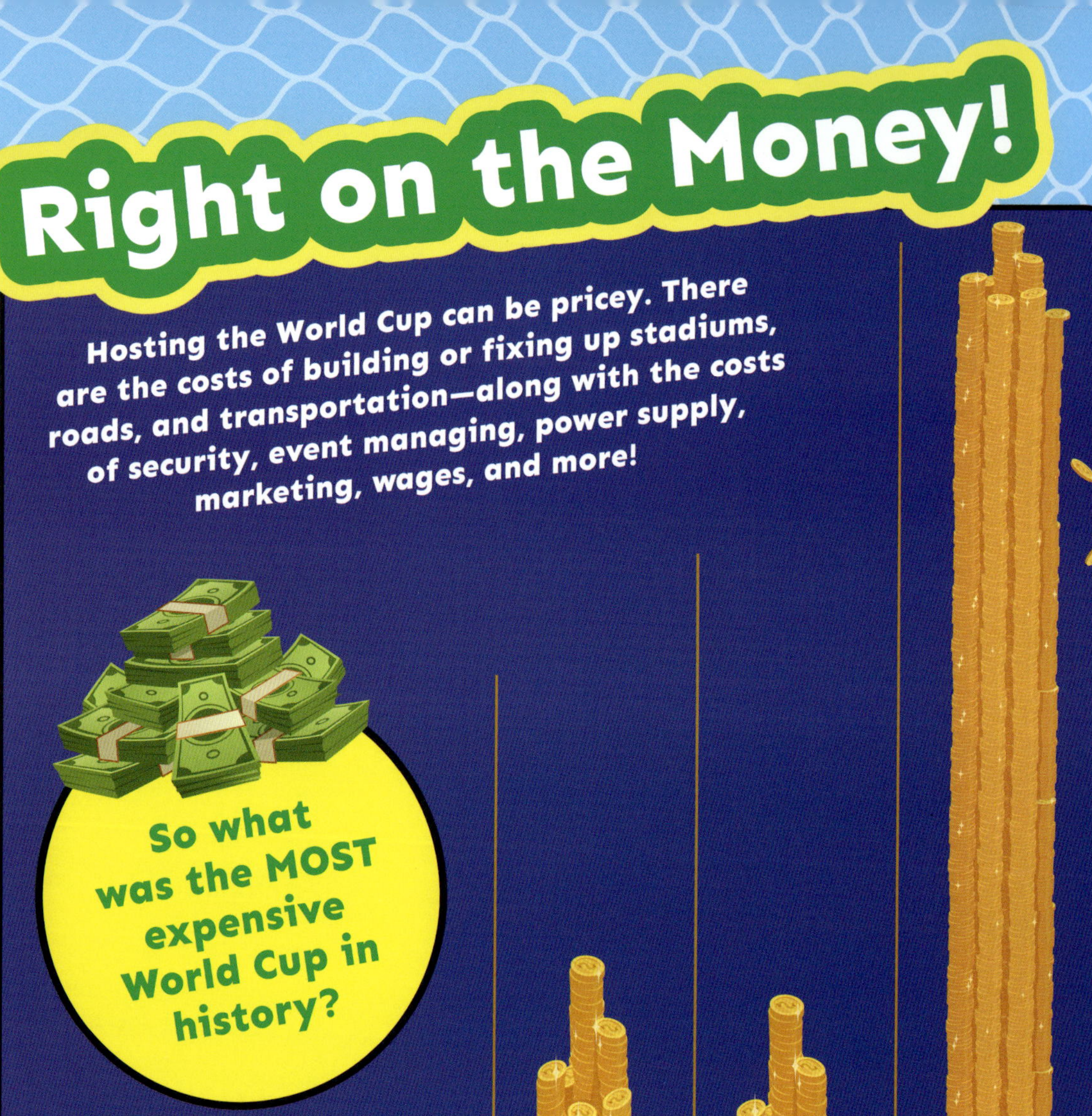

HOST COUNTRY	South Africa	Brazil	Russia	Qatar
YEAR	2010	2014	2018	2022
COST IN BILLION US DOLLARS	$3.6	$15	$11.6	$220

Players may play to win . . . but they also make bank.

Here are the top $$$$ prizes from the 2022 World Cup.

2022 PRIZE MONEY (USD)	
Winning Team	**$42 MILLION**
Second place team	**$30 MILLION**
Third Place	**$27 MILLION**
Fourth Place	**$25 MILLION**
Each of the four teams knocked out in the quarterfinals	**$17 MILLION**
Each of the eight teams knocked out in the Round of 16	**$14 MILLION**
Each of the 16 teams knocked out at the group stage	**$9 MILLION**

HOW DOES THAT STACK UP?
The USMNT earned almost as much for *qualifying* for the 2022 World Cup ($9 mil) as the US Women's National Team made for *winning* their 2023 World Cup ($10.5 mil).

PART 3: WORLD CUP MEMORABLE MOMENTS

The Biggest Upsets in World Cup History

A soccer game is never over until it's over. Here are some iconic World Cup moments that made history—and surprised fans!

EL MARACANAZO ("THE MARACANÃ BLOW"), 1950

The 1950 Brazilian National Team was used to beating Uruguay. They entered Maracanã Stadium in Rio de Janeiro ready to do it again—with more than 200,000 confident fans cheering them on. Bets were made. Songs were written. Then . . . Uruguay won 2–1. And the nation was shaken!

GEOFF HURST'S "PHANTOM GOAL," 1966

Hat trick or trick of the eye? English forward Geoff Hurst gets credit for a third goal he didn't actually score—footage later shows it bouncing off the goalpost—but it's 1966 and there's no tech so England advances and Germany says, "Auf Wiedersehen."

What would YOU add to the list?

- Germany beats Brazil 7–1 in 2014?
- Saudi Arabia beats Argentina 2–1 in their opening game in 2022?
- Algeria's 2–1 victory over Germany in 1982?
- Cameroon's 1–0 win over world champions Argentina in 1990?
- Or North Korea's 1–0 win over Italy in 1966?

THE "MIRACLE ON GRASS," 1950

England's players were the "Kings of Football," the best in the sport, and favored to win the trophy. The US team had trained together only once before the tournament. The US didn't have a chance . . . until they won, 1–0, and sent England home.

BAGGIO MISSES THE PENALTY, 1994

Roberto Baggio was one of the best players of his generation—known for the incredible accuracy of his free kicks. But the defining moment of his career was when he *missed* the shot during the penalty shoot-out that ended the 1994 World Cup final. Italy lost to Brazil, 1–0.

THE GOLDEN GENERATION: Hungary's 1954 National Team scored more goals in a single World Cup tournament—27—than any other team in history!

THE MIRACLE OF BERN, 1954

West Germany beats the *heavily* favored Hungarian team in the eighty-sixth minute of their first World Cup game after World War II. How'd they do it? Some credit the removable studs on their cleats for helping them zip ahead on a muddy field!

World Cup Superstitions

Soccer is full of superstitions: fans who won't wash their lucky socks before a game, players who always have to enter the field on the same foot, and even coaches who won't let players eat chicken!

NATIONAL NOTIONS!

The Brazilian national team walks onto the field holding hands for good luck.

The 1962 Chilean national team snacked on their opponent's national food or drink before each game for good luck.

Japan's national team switched from red-and-white uniforms to blue-and-white when they didn't qualify for both the 1990 World Cup and the 1992 Summer Olympics. Was the fix about the fit or superstition?

The 1998 French national team had lots of superstitious rituals. For luck, the players always sat in the same seats on their bus, and they listened to Gloria Gaynor's song "I Will Survive" in the locker room before every game.

FUN FACT! 1998 French captain, **Laurent Blanc**, kissed goalkeeper Fabien Barthez's bald head before *every* game of the 1998 World Cup—and the team went on to win the trophy!

Ronaldo's Rituals

Portuguese striker Cristiano Ronaldo likes to be the last player out of the tunnel before a match and always steps onto the field with his right foot first.

Neymar's Hair

Brazilian superstar Neymar flew his hairdresser to Qatar to dye his hair blond before his team's 2022 group stage game against South Korea. Why? He wanted to sport the same style he wore when he scored a brace against South Korea in a June 2022 friendly.

The Curse of the Host Nation

Many host nations have *not* done well over the years. In fact, since 1966 no host nation has made it past the quarterfinals. Is it the pressure of high expectations . . . or a curse?

Big Yikes!

Dutch soccer legend Johan Cruyff, who retired in 1984, slapped his goalkeeper on the stomach before every game—and spit out his chewing gum onto the opponent's half of the field.

Grossest Superstition

Argentina's 1990 World Cup goalkeeper, Sergio Goycochea, urinated on the pitch before every penalty shoot-out. The first time was out of necessity, but then the team won so he kept doing it. Ick!

Pelé's Jersey

Legendary Brazilian player Pelé blamed a slump on a jersey he gave to a fan—so he sent a friend to get it back. As soon as he started wearing the jersey again, his game got better!

Messi's Mornings

During the 2022 World Cup, Messi and teammate Rodrigo De Paul drank maté (a kind of tea) together in Messi's hotel room every morning at exactly 9:30. And Messi got mad if De Paul was late!

SUPERSTITION OR STRATEGY? Lionel Messi walks around the middle of the field before each game to calm himself and think over his opponents' strengths and weaknesses.

Goals, Glorious Goals!

A goal is scored by getting the whole ball past the goal line and into the goal—*without* any fouls. And while scoring goals is the *goal* of every soccer game, it's way harder than it seems. Luckily, every World Cup is full of awe-inspiring goals. Here are a few standouts!

1986: MARADONA'S "Goal of the Century" Against England

Only four minutes after his career-defining foul, Maradona sprinted sixty yards in ten seconds, dribbling past three English players and their goalie, to score the most beautiful goal of his career—and a win for Argentina in the quarterfinals!

Fellow **Argentine Lionel Messi** is also known for dribbling around opponents to score beautiful goals. Here he is scoring his third goal in the second half of extra time in the 2022 final against **France**.

TIME OUT FOR TRIVIA!

How big is a World Cup goal?

Answer: The goalposts are 24 feet apart and the crossbar is 8 feet above the ground.

2002: **Ahn Jung-hwan's Golden Goal Against Italy**

South Korea's forward beats **Italian** GOAT **Paolo Maldini** to a cross and scores on a header. South Korea advances to the semifinals and Italy says, "Ciao!"

FUN FACT! Jung-hwan was kicked off his Italian club team—Perugia—for sending Italy home!

GOALS BY THE NUMBERS

172

MOST GOALS SCORED IN A WORLD CUP

2022 in Qatar

12

HIGHEST SCORING WORLD CUP MATCH OF ALL TIME

7–5 Austria v Switzerland, 1954 quarterfinals

7

MOST GOALS SCORED IN A WORLD CUP FINAL

Brazil v Sweden, 5–2, 1958

TIME OUT FOR TRIVIA!

Who was the highest scoring World Cup team of all time with a total of 229 goals?

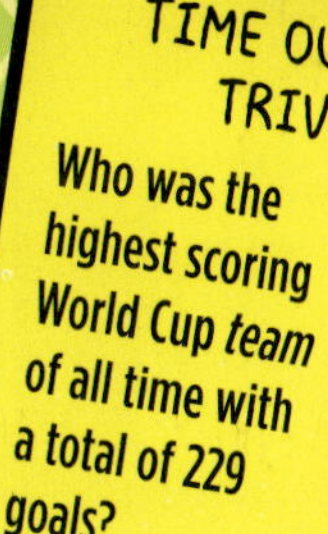

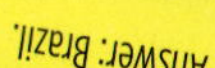

Answer: Brazil!

RECORD-BREAKERS!

Just Fontaine of France (1958) holds the record for most goals scored by one player in a World Cup tournament: 13 goals in 6 matches!

Miroslav Klose of Germany (2001–2014) holds the record for most goals scored overall in World Cup history: 16 goals in 4 tournaments.

Asamoah Gyan of Ghana (2003–2009) is the only player outside of Europe and South America to score more than 5 goals at a World Cup tournament!

The Most Memorable Goal Celebrations of All Time!

From dances to fist pumping to heart hands to sliding into the corner with their arms out wide, soccer players find lots of ways to show off their style when celebrating a goal!

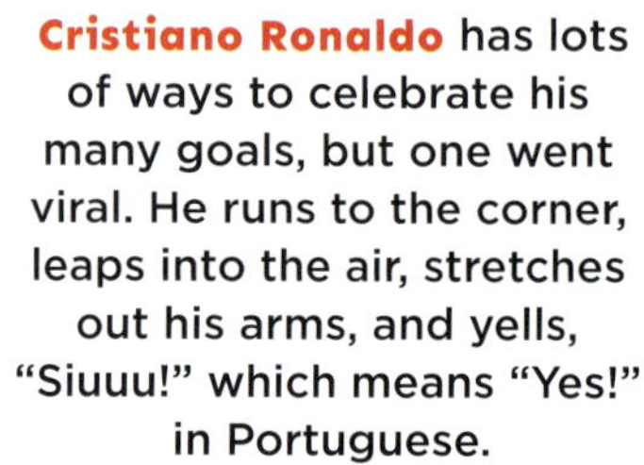
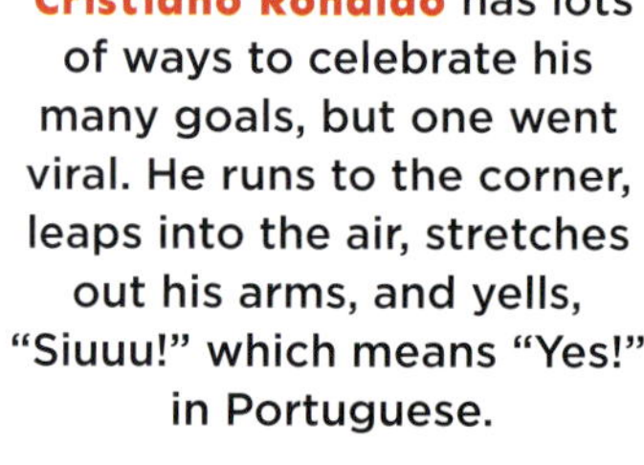

Cristiano Ronaldo has lots of ways to celebrate his many goals, but one went viral. He runs to the corner, leaps into the air, stretches out his arms, and yells, "Siuuu!" which means "Yes!" in Portuguese.

Lionel Messi dedicates every goal to his maternal grandmother by pointing two fingers to the sky. She took him to his first practices as a kid and argued with the coach who thought he was way too short to play.

Ireland's **Robbie Keane** scored a record sixty-eight goals for the Republic of Ireland—and did a sloppy cartwheel every single time!

38-year-old striker **Robert Milla** of **Cameroon** scored four goals in the 1990 World Cup—and celebrated each one by dancing his "Makossa" for fans in front of the corner flag.

"Milla's Makossa" was immediately imitated/adopted/mimicked/used by players all over the world!

Uruguayan forward **Edinson Cavani's** trademark bow-and-arrow celebration is in honor of his country's indigenous people.

Brazilian football legend **Ronaldo** celebrated goals with the "shhh" gesture.

Bafétimbi Gomis of France, aka "the Black Panther," crawled and clawed like a panther after every goal.

After scoring in the 1982 final against West Germany, Italian **Marco Tardelli** ran toward the Italian bench screaming "Gol! Gol!"—and it became one of the most iconic moments in World Cup history!

Sometimes French superstar **Kylian Mbappé** jumps up in the air, then crosses his arms across his chest and tucks his hands under his armpits in his signature "Hibiscus" or "Calma" celebration.

Dutch defender **Virgil van Dijk** favors the classic "rock on" hand gesture.

South Korea's **Son Heung-min** does camera celebrations after scoring.

Norway's star striker, **Erling Haaland** has plenty of ways to celebrate goals, and his meditative lotus pose—showing off his inner peace and calm—is his most iconic celebration.

Julius Aghahowa did seven backflips when he scored Nigeria's only goal in the 2002 World Cup.

Many players like Egyptian forward **Mohamed Salah** show thanks to God after a goal.

GOAL!

Polish forward **Robert Lewandowski** celebrates his goals by pressing his clenched fists together in front of his chest. The meaning is a secret between him and his daughter.

Goalkeepers Hall of Fame

The goalkeeper has the most intense job in soccer! He has to block shots, win the ball in the air, and organize the team's defense. A truly *great* goalie can even start a play that leads to a goal. Here are some grand goalies and their spectacular saves!

"THE SAVE OF THE CENTURY"

One of the greatest goalies of all time, **Gordon Bank** of England, made a legendary save against Pelé's powerful header in the 1970 World Cup.

Argentina's **Emiliano Martinez**'s historic save in the 123rd minute of the 2022 World Cup final helped Argentina make it to the penalty shoot-out—and the victory!

PENALTY SHOOT-OUT

Goalkeepers have to read the shooter's subtle body language to know which direction to dive during a penalty shoot-out.

Yann Summer sizes up **Bryan Ruiz**.

Gianluigi Buffon makes a save in the 2006 final that keeps **Italy** in the game. They go on to win the World Cup in a penalty shoot-out!

Iker Casillas—the goalie of **Spain's** "Golden Era" (2008–2012)—helped Spain win the World Cup in 2010.

More Goalkeeper Glory!

Manueal Neuer made the sweeper keeper role mainstream when he helped Germany win the 2014 World Cup, but it was Lev Yashin—legendary Russian goalkeeper of the 1950s and 60s—who invented it.

WHAT'S A SWEEPER KEEPER? Sweeper keepers don't wait for danger to come to them. They take a more active role to "sweep up" danger outside their penalty box—sometimes up to 40 feet past the goal. To do that, they have to be good with their feet, able to receive the ball under pressure, and to make accurate passes to defenders and midfielders.

PLAY BY THE RULES! Sure, goalkeepers can use their hands—but only for six seconds and only inside their penalty area. They can't pick it up on a throw-in or when a teammate passes the ball back to them!

FUN FACT!
#ThingsTimHowardCouldSave trended for weeks afterward!

RECORD-BREAKING SAVES

USA goalie **Tim Howard** made a record-breaking 16 saves in the USA's 2014 Round-of-16 game against Belgium—the most saves ever in one WC game!

Hugo Lloris of France holds the record for most World Cup matches played by a goalkeeper. His 20th was the 2022 final against Argentina!

Goalkeepers **Peter Shilton** of England and **Fabien Barthez** of France share the record for most clean sheets in a World Cup tournament—with 10 clean sheets out of 17 games each!

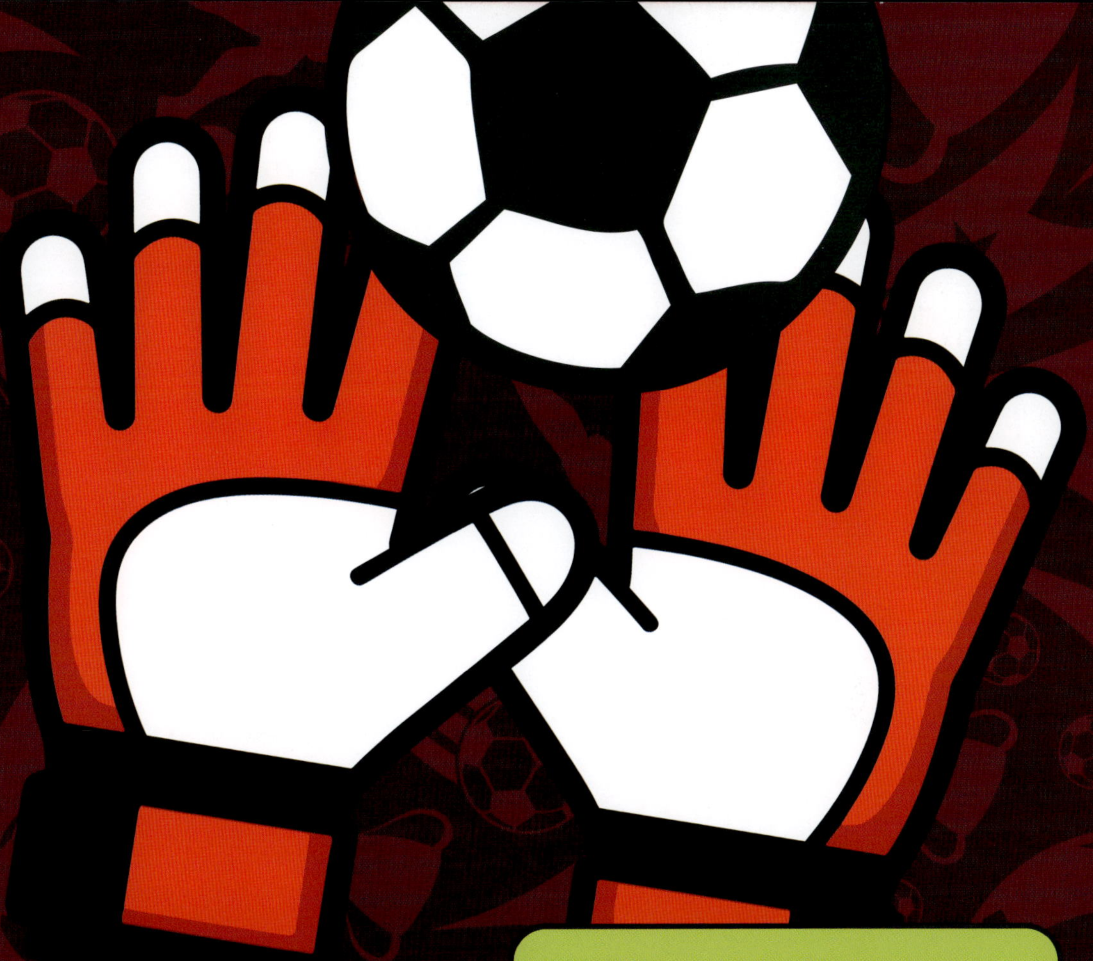

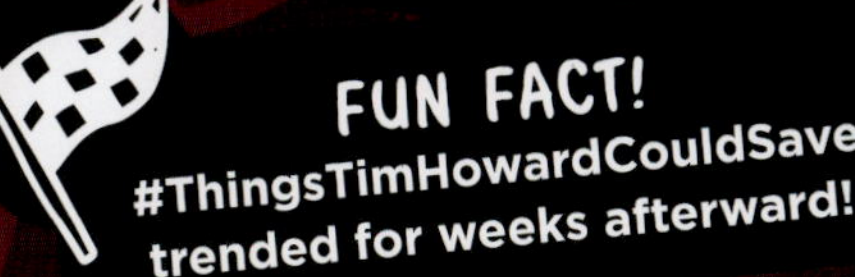

WHAT'S A CLEAN SHEET? It's a shutout! And it happens when the goalie—and the defense—keep the other team from scoring for the whole game. The longest any goalkeeper has gone without letting in a goal during the World Cup is **518 minutes**, and it happened in 1990. Gloves off to Italy's **Walter Zenga**, the Italian goalkeeper who set that record.

The Road to the World Cup

In soccer, all the national teams are broken into six "confederations" by region or continent. Each confederation gets to send a certain number of teams to the World Cup. And each confederation holds its own competitions or "qualifiers" to decide who gets to play in the World Cup!

FUN FACT!
Host countries automatically qualify for the World Cup!

CONCACAF
Confederation of North, Central America, and Caribbean Association Football
6 TEAMS

CONMEBOL
South American Football Confederation
6 TEAMS

WILD CARDS! The **Inter-Confederation Playoffs** decide the last two World Cup spots! UEFA teams don't participate—they already have the most slots!

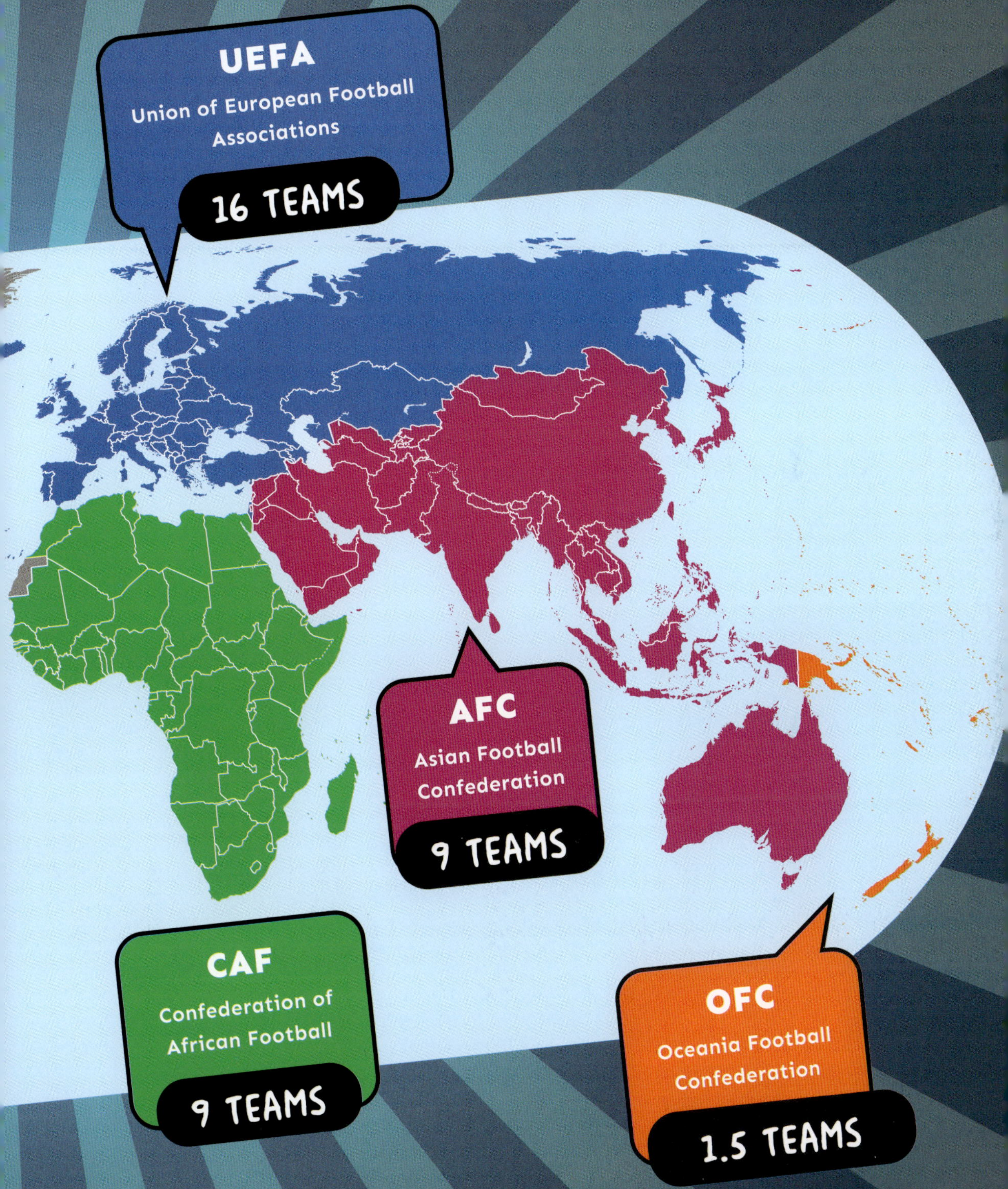

UEFA
Union of European Football Associations
16 TEAMS

AFC
Asian Football Confederation
9 TEAMS

CAF
Confederation of African Football
9 TEAMS

OFC
Oceania Football Confederation
1.5 TEAMS

PART 4: THE TEAMS

CONCACAF

The Confederation of North, Central America, and Caribbean Association Football

Forty-one national teams play in CONCACAF but only eight get to go to the World Cup. The top two runners-up will get to compete in the Inter-Confederation playoffs for the final two World Cup slots.

CANADA

MEXICO

UNITED STATES

In 2026, **3 out of 6** CONCACAF World Cup slots go to the host countries!

BELIZE

COSTA RICA

EL SALVADOR

GUATEMALA

HONDURAS

NICARAGUA

PANAMA

ANGUILLA

ANTIGUA AND BARBUDA

ARUBA

BAHAMAS

BARBADOS

BERMUDA

BONAIRE

BRITISH VIRGIN ISLANDS

CAYMAN ISLANDS

CUBA

CURAÇAO

DOMINICA

DOMINICAN REPUBLIC

FRENCH GUIANA

GRENADA

GUADELOUPE

GUYANA

HAITI

JAMAICA

MARTINIQUE

MONTSERRAT

PUERTO RICO

SAINT KITTS AND NEVIS

SAINT LUCIA

SAINT MARTIN

SAINT VINCENT AND THE GRENADINES

SINT MAARTEN

SURINAME

TRINIDAD AND TOBAGO

TURKS AND CAICOS ISLANDS

U.S. VIRGIN ISLANDS

One Nation. One Team.

Meet the United States Men's National Team

TEAM NICKNAMES:
"The Yanks"
and "The Stars and Stripes"

HEAD COACH:
Mauricio Pochettino

BIGGEST RIVAL:
Mexico

BEST FINISH:
Semifinals/Third Place 1930

SECOND-BEST FINISH:
Quarterfinals 2002

FUN FACT! The US did not qualify for a single World Cup between 1950 and 1990.

WELCOME, MAURICIO POCHETTINO!

The US Men's National Team hasn't made it past the World Cup's Round of 16 since 2002. But that's about to change! With high-profile coach Mauricio Pochettino in charge, the 2026 World Cup is bound to be the USA's most memorable tournament ever!

FUN FACT! The US has played in 11 out of 22 Men's World Cups.

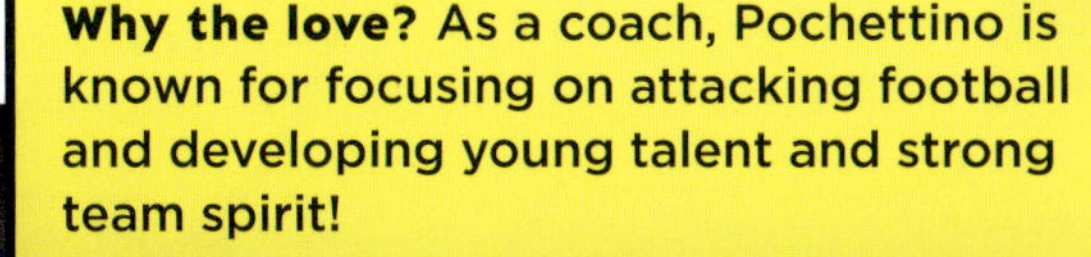

Why the love? As a coach, Pochettino is known for focusing on attacking football and developing young talent and strong team spirit!

As a player, he played defense for the Argentine national team in twenty games—including at the 2002 World Cup!

FUN FACT! He got his start in soccer playing for the same club as Lionel Messi: Newell's Old Boys!

TIME OUT FOR TRIVIA!

Which USMNT coach racked up more wins than any other and led the team to the quarterfinals? Was it Bob Bradley, Bruce Arenas, Jürgen Klinsmann, or Gregg Berhalter?

Answer: Bruce Arenas!

Star Power

In summer 2026, all eyes will be on #10, forward **CHRISTIAN PULISIC**. He's one of the top five USMNT goal scorers *of all* time and top ten for assists, meaning he made the last pass or play before the goal was scored.

NICKNAME: Captain America

JERSEY #: 10

POSITION: Forward

BIRTHDAY: September 18, 1998

HOMETOWN: Hershey, PA

HEIGHT: 5′ 10″

CLUB: AC MILAN (ITALY)

Pulisic made his debut with the national team when he was 17 years and 192 days old and became the youngest USMNT player to play in a World Cup qualifying game.

The US won that game against Guatemala, 4–0!

He's been US Player of the Year 4 times—just like USA GOAT, Landon Donovan!

At 20 years, 189 days old, he became the youngest USMNT player to score 10 international goals!

Pulisic was also the youngest captain in USMNT history in 2018 at 20 years old.

PULISIC'S ALL-STAR TEAMMATES

Defender **Antonee "Jedi" Robinson**

High-energy midfielder **Weston McKennie**

Creative midfielder **Yunus Musah**

Top attacking talent **Tim Weah**

Who would YOU add to the list?

- Defensive midfielder Tyler Adams?
- Savvy striker Ricardo Pepi?
- Midfielder Gio Reyna?
- Goalkeeper Matt Turner?
- Or another rising star?

Pulisic scores an epic game-winning goal against **Iran** in 2022.

Top Moments in USMNT History

1 LANDON DONOVAN'S LEGENDARY GOAL AGAINST ALGERIA, 2010

The USMNT finishes at the top of their group for the first time in history thanks to Landon Donovan's ninety-first minute goal against Algeria.

"IT MADE US BELIEVE." —LANDON DONOVAN

2 PAUL CALIGIURI'S "SHOT HEARD AROUND THE WORLD," 1989

Paul Caligiuri's iconic goal in a qualifying match against Trinidad and Tobago not only landed the United States a spot in the 1990 World Cup—their first appearance since 1950—but boosted soccer's popularity in the US and led to the first US gig as hosts in 1994!

What would YOU add to the list?

Jermaine Jones's missile-like corner kick against Portugal in 2014?

Earnie Stewart's 1994 goal against Colombia that helped get the US to the Round of 16 for the first time?

Or goalkeeper Tim Howard's record-breaking 16 saves against Belgium in 2014?

3

"DOS A CERO!" 2002

Landon Donovan scores on a header in the sixty-fifth minute to clinch the US 2–0 win over Mexico—sending the USMNT into the quarterfinals for the first time since 1930. Their victory sparks a chant that fans still use to taunt their rivals!

FUN FACT! No other CONCACAF team has reached the World Cup semifinals since!

4

THE 1930 WORLD CUP

The US finishes in third place—their best standing ever—and American striker Bert Patenaude scores the first-ever hat trick at a World Cup.

The 1930 team was nicknamed the shot-putters because they'd send the ball long instead of relying on short passes to move it up the field.

5

THE MIRACLE ON GRASS, 1950

A ragtag US team full of accountants, teachers, plumbers, and restaurant workers knocks England out of the World Cup.

Best USMNT Players of All-Time

TOP THREE ALL-TIME LEADING GOAL SCORERS

1. **Landon Donovan:** 57 goals
2. **Clint Dempsey:** 57 goals
3. **Jozy Altidore:** 42 goals

USMNT ALL-TIME BEST GOALKEEPERS

1. **Tim Howard**
2. **Kasey Keller**
3. **Tony Meola**

MOST APPEARANCES IN USMNT HISTORY

1. **Cobi Jones,** 164
2. **Landon Donovan,** 157
3. **Michael Bradley,** 151

If you *HAD* to pick the Top Ten USMNT Players of All Time:

- Landon Donovan
- Clint Dempsey
- Claudio Reyna
- Tim Howard
- Eric Wynalda
- Brad Friedel
- Michael Bradley
- Brian McBride
- Cobi Jones
- Christian Pulisic

Who would YOU add to or take off the list?

USMNT GOATS

LANDON DONOVAN (2000–2014)

A legend for leadership, goal scoring, and playing well under pressure, Landon Donovan has been the face of the USMNT and Major League Soccer for more than a decade.

BIRTH DATE: March 4, 1982

HOMETOWN: Ontario, CA

JERSEY #: 10

POSITION: Forward and attacking midfielder

INTERNATIONAL GOALS: 57

INTERNATIONAL ASSISTS: 58

INTERNATIONAL APPEARANCES: 157

WORLD CUPS PLAYED: 2002, 2006, 2010

CAREER HIGHLIGHT: 2010 stoppage-time goal against Algeria

BIGGEST DISAPPOINTMENT: Not making it onto the 2014 World Cup roster

RECORDS

- Tied for top USMNT goal scorer!
- Holds record for most assists!
- 2002 Best Young Player of the World Cup.
- The youngest player in USMNT history to play in international competition 50 times.
- Elected to US Men's Soccer Hall of Fame in 2023.

TIME OUT FOR TRIVIA!

Donovan's soccer career isn't over just because he's no longer on the field. He's a commentator and has a podcast with Tim Howard. Can you name any other USMNT stars who have podcasts, YouTube shows, or regular gigs as TV or radio commentators?

Answer: Alexi Lalas, Clint Dempsey, Taylor Twellman, Cobi Jones, Tony Meola, Kasey Keller, DaMarcus Beasley, Oguchi Onyewu, and Marcelo Balboa—just to name a few!

CLINT DEMPSEY (2004–2017)

Known for his grit, aggressive style of play, and spectacular goals, Clint Dempsey helped define US soccer for a generation.

BIRTH DATE: March 9, 1983

HOMETOWN: NACOGDOCHES, TX

JERSEY #: 8

POSITION: Forward and midfielder

INTERNATIONAL GOALS: 57

INTERNATIONAL ASSISTS: 21

INTERNATIONAL APPEARANCES: 141 games

WORLD CUPS PLAYED: 2006, 2010, 2014

CAREER HIGHLIGHT: Broke his nose in the USMNT's 2014 opening game, then came back to score against Portugal in the very next game for a 2–2 draw

BIGGEST DISAPPOINTMENT: Didn't qualify for the 2018 World Cup

RECORDS

- Tied for top USMNT goal scorer!
- Captained the squad for the 2014 World Cup!
- Became the first USMNT player to score in 3 different World Cups!
- Ranked fourth in most games played with USMNT!
- Scored US's fastest World Cup goal in 2014 against Ghana—just 29 seconds into their opening game (the fifth fastest in tournament history)!
- Inducted into US SOCCER HALL OF FAME IN 2022.

The Timeline of a Goal: 2010 USA v Algeria, 1–0

In a wild ending to a high-stakes game, the US advanced to the Round of 16 on one of its best goals ever. Here's the breakdown!

WHAT'S AT STAKE? Only one team can make it out of the group stage into the Round of 16. The USA had to win. All Algeria had to do was tie.

90 minutes

+4 minutes of stoppage time are added to the clock.

- Algerian striker **Rafik Saïfi** heads the ball toward the goal.
- Blocked by US goalkeeper **Tim Howard**!
- **Landon Donovan** starts running—*hard*—from the midfield.
- **Howard** pushes forward. He throws the ball in the path of a sprinting **Donovan**.
- **Jozy Altidore** and **Clint Dempsey** run up the wings (the sides of the field).
- **Donovan** plays the ball to **Jozy Altidore**, who's out wide right.

Minute 91

The ball hits the back of the net.

Gooooal!

- **Donovan's** teammates pile on top of him in celebration!

Minute 93

- Algerian defender **Antar Yahia** gets his second yellow card of the game. No one else scores.

- **Donovan** never stops running.
- **Altidore** crosses the ball to Dempsey, who's wide left.
- **Donovan** keeps running.
- **Dempsey** takes the shot.
- It's blocked by Algerian goalkeeper, **Raïs M'Bolhi**—but it bounces away!
- **Donovan** is already there—a few feet in front of the goal—ready for the rebound. He runs onto the ball.

- Post-Game Celebration: Former US President **Bill Clinton** comes to the locker room to congratulate the team and later joins them at their hotel to celebrate.

Minute 94

Game Over! USMNT history is made! The US advances to the Round of 16!

The Aftermath:

FANDEMONIUM!
US soccer fans, newbies, and naysayers across the country hug, cheer, and rally behind the USMNT!

CONCACAF

HOST COUNTRY!

MEXICO

FUN FACT! Mexico has host luck! They hosted in 1970 and 1986 and made it to the quarterfinals both times! How far will the team go in 2026?

TEAM NICKNAME: "El Tri" (short for "el tricolor") after the Mexican flag

CAPTAIN: Edson Álvarez, midfielder

PREVIOUS WORLD CUPS PLAYED: 1930, 1950, 1954, 1958, 1962, 1966, 1970, 1978, 1986, 1990, 1994, 1998, 2002, 2006, 2010, 2014, 2018, 2022

HIGHEST RANKING/STAGE/ROUND: Quarterfinals

MEXICO'S HALL OF FAME

Manuel Negrete's legendary scissor-kick goal against **Bulgaria** during their 1986 quarterfinal match is one of the best World Cup goals in history!

PLAYERS TO WATCH!

Forward **Santiago Giménez** hugs star striker **Raúl Jiménez** during the CONCACAF Nations League semifinal match with **Canada. Mexico** went on to win the tournament!

Who are the Top Three Mexican players of all time?

1. Hugo Sánchez (1977–1994)
2. Cuauhtémoc Blanco (1995–2010)
3. Rafael Márquez (1997–2018)

DO YOU AGREE?

Who would **YOU** add to the list?

CONCACAF

CANADA

HOST COUNTRY!

TEAM NICKNAME: "The Canucks" and "Les Rouges" ("The Reds")

CAPTAIN: Alphonso Davies, Left-back

PREVIOUS WORLD CUPS PLAYED: 1986, 2022

HIGHEST RANKING/STAGE/ROUND: Group Stage

Team photo from June 2024 friendly match against the **Panama National Team**.

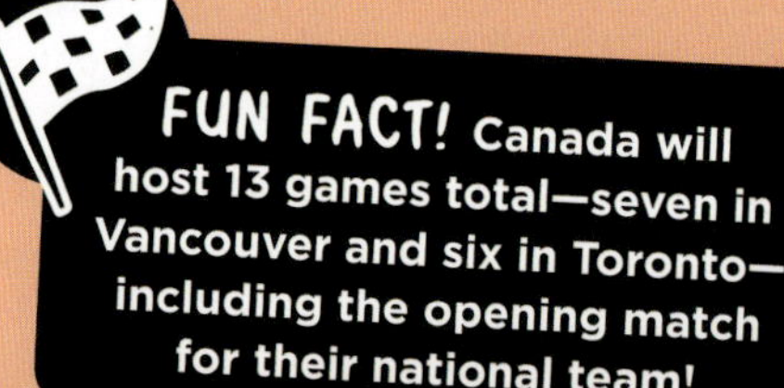

FUN FACT! Canada will host 13 games total—seven in Vancouver and six in Toronto—including the opening match for their national team!

FUN FACT! Canada had a 17-year losing streak against the USA (1991-2016) but that's all changing with Canada's superstar roster!

Who are the greatest Canadian soccer players of all time?

1. Jonathan David
2. Alphonso Davies
3. Atiba Hutchinson!

Canada's **Ali Ahmed** #20 battles the **Ivory Coast**'s **Ghislain Konan** in their International Friendly match in June 2025.

PLAYERS TO WATCH!

Canadian superstar **Alphonso Davies** (defender, forward, and midfielder) scoring Canada's first-ever World Cup goal in 2022.

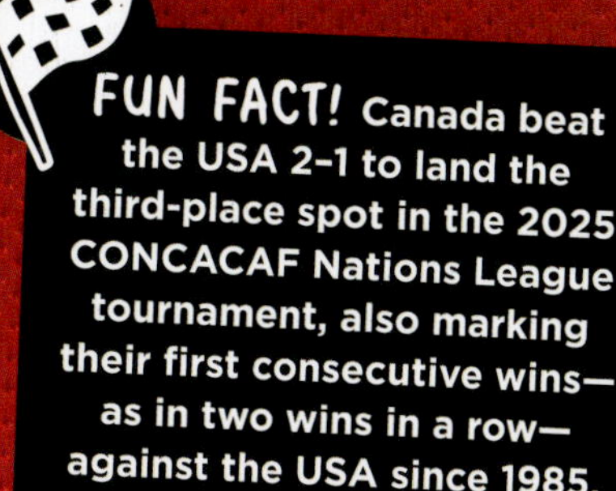

FUN FACT! Canada beat the USA 2-1 to land the third-place spot in the 2025 CONCACAF Nations League tournament, also marking their first consecutive wins—as in two wins in a row—against the USA since 1985.

MÉXICO
USA

What's the biggest rivalry in CONCACAF?

THE USA v MEXICO!

While Mexico lost only one game to the USA between 1937 and 1980, the rivalry heated up when the USA won their Round-of-16 match in the 2002 World Cup and sent Mexico packing! Since then, the USA and Mexico have vied for top team in CONCACAF tournaments.

The two countries also share a border—*and fans*! In US states like California and Texas, where lots of families have Mexican heritage, there are tons of fans for *both* national teams. Another touchy subject? Fighting over top players who are citizens of both the US *and* Mexico!

TEAM TO WATCH: PANAMA

In 2025, **Panama** surprised soccer fans at the 2025 CONCACAF Nations League by beating the **US** to face off against **Mexico** in the final!

CONCACAF

Team Highlights!

JAMAICAN midfielder, THEODORE WHITMORE scored two goals against JAPAN to win their group stage match.

The team's nickname is the "Reggae Boyz!"

HISTORY MAKERS!

In 1998, JAMAICA became the first Caribbean nation to qualify for the World Cup.

HONDURAS made it to the World Cup in 1982, 2010, and 2014. How far will they go in 2026?

In 2014, underdog **COSTA RICA** made history and toppled their "group of death," besting Uruguay, Italy, and England—three former World Cup winners!

FUN FACT! Costa Rica scored *three* goals for the first time in a World Cup match.

#23 FELIPE BALOY scores **PANAMA**'s first goal in their first World Cup against **ENGLAND** in 2018.

WAIT! "GROUP OF DEATH?" WHAT?

It's when almost all the teams in the group are really strong, which makes it harder for anyone to advance. In 2014, the US went up against Germany, Portugal, and Ghana!

The UEFA nations will send sixteen teams to the 2026 World Cup and do not play in the Inter-Confederation playoffs. How do they decide who goes? All 55 member nations are split into twelve groups of four or five teams where everyone plays each other twice. The twelve group winners go to the World Cup, and the remaining sixteen teams battle it out for the four remaining spots.

Who's a member? Check it out!

ALBANIA

ANDORRA

ARMENIA

AUSTRIA

AZERBAIJAN

BELARUS

BELGIUM

BOSNIA AND HERZEGOVINA

BULGARIA

GERMANY

GIBRALTAR

GREECE

HUNGARY

ICELAND

ISRAEL

ITALY

KAZAKHSTAN

KOSOVO

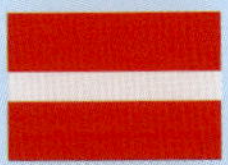

LATVIA

LIECHTENSTEIN

LITHUANIA

LUXEMBOURG

MALTA

MOLDOVA

MONTENEGRO

NETHERLANDS

NORTH MACEDONIA

NORTHERN IRELAND

NORWAY

POLAND

PORTUGAL

REPUBLIC OF IRELAND

ROMANIA

RUSSIA

SAN MARINO

SCOTLAND

SERBIA

SLOVAKIA

SLOVENIA

SPAIN

SWEDEN

SWITZERLAND

TURKEY

UKRAINE

WALES

UEFA World Cup Wins!

France, led by team captain **Kylian Mbappé**, wins in 2018.

Spain's Golden Generation takes home the trophy in 2010.

Netherlands made it to the final three times—in 1974, 1978, and 2010!

Hungary made it to the final twice—in 1938 and 1954!

Czechoslovakia made it to the final twice—in 1934 and 1962!

Sweden made it to the final in 1958!

Croatia made it to the final in 2018!

UEFA

Memorable Moments

BIGGEST EUROPEAN RIVALRY IN HISTORY!

With so many powerhouse teams, it's no surprise that there are *a lot* of long-standing rivalries in the UEFA—such as Serbia v Croatia, England v Germany, and Spain v Portugal.

But the biggest of all may be **Germany v the Netherlands**. Both teams have been top ranked for years, but the roots of the rivalry go back to World War II when Germany occupied the Netherlands.

 V 

FUN FACT! In 2018 and 2022, the defending German champions were eliminated in the group stage!

GERMANY holds the record for most consecutive World Cup games without a defeat: 18 wins and 3 draws from 1982 to 2002.

Iceland made it to the World Cup in 2018, where the team and fans celebrated with a Viking Thunder Clap!

The 1974 **Netherlands** team invented and perfected total football. Here, **Dutch** midfielder **Johan Cruyff** dribbles past **Argentinian** goalkeeper **Daniel Carnevali** to score during their 1974 quarterfinal match.

What's Tiki-Taka?
A kind of precise passing that helped Spain's Golden Generation win three consecutive major international tournaments—including the 2010 World Cup!

UNDERDOGS FOR THE WIN!

BULGARIA took down Germany in the 1994 quarterfinals in one of the biggest upsets in European World Cup history!

REPUBLIC OF IRELAND beat Italy in their 1994 opening match.

In their first World Cup ever, **UKRAINE** went all the way to the 2006 quarterfinals with an epic penalty shoot-out win against Switzerland in the Round of 16!

UEFA

Memorable Moments

SPECTACULAR GOALS

Dutch striker **Robin van Persie**'s 2014 diving header against one of the best goalies of all time, **Spain**'s **Iker Castillas**, became known as the "Flying Dutchman."

POLAND finished third in 1974 and 1982 during their "golden era."

WALES made it to the quarterfinals in 1958. They lost to Brazil in the match where a young Pelé scored his first international goal!

AUSTRIA has played in the World Cup seven times. Their best performance came in 1954, when they landed third place. They have not qualified for any tournament since 1998. Will 2026 be their year?

MIRACULOUS COMEBACK!
Belgium's 3–2 win against **Japan** in the 2018 Round of 16 sent them to the quarterfinals—and it's one of the greatest comebacks in World Cup history! **Nacer Chadli** scored the winning goal in extra time.

EUROPE'S TOP FIVE GOAL SCORERS IN WORLD CUP HISTORY:

1. Miroslav Klose (Germany): 16 goals
2. Gerd Müller (Germany): 14 goals
3. Just Fontaine (France): 13 goals
4. Kylian Mbappé (France): 12 goals
5. Sándor Kocsis (Hungary) and Jürgen Klinsmann (Germany): 11 goals

Cristiano Ronaldo of **Portugal** nets an amazing hat trick against **Spain** in their 2018 group stage match that he finishes off with a stunning free kick.

IT'S ALL IN THE NAME!
Both the Welsh and Slovenian national teams are nicknamed the Dragons. Kazakhstan's team nickname is the Snow Leopards and Montenegro's is the Brave Falcons!

UEFA

Players to Watch

From returning greats to rising stars, here are some of the many UEFA players to look out for in the 2026 World Cup.

PORTUGAL

CRISTIANO RONALDO may be forty years old but he's still got a shot at bringing home the trophy for **PORTUGAL**.

Or will younger players like **JOÃO NEVES** shine?

FRANCE

KYLIAN MBAPPÉ: Did somebody say goals? **FRANCE**'s team captain, Kylian Mbappé, is one of the fastest players and top goal scorers in the world.

ANTOINE GREIZMANN: Veteran midfielder and one of the greatest players of his generation.

KARIM BENZEMA: He's scored more than five hundred career goals for club and country.

SPAIN

PEDRI (PEDRO GONZÁLEZ LÓPEZ): Midfielder known for his exceptional playmaking.

RODRI (RODRIGO HERNÁNDEZ CASCANTE): One of the best defensive midfielders in the world.

LAMINE YAMAL: At fifteen, he became the youngest player to debut on the world stage in almost a century. Can he become one of the greats?

GERMANY

FLORIAN WIRTZ is widely regarded as one of the best attacking midfielders in the world.

POLAND

POLAND's top goal scorer, **ROBERT LEWANDOWSKI**, will be back in 2026!

ENGLAND

HARRY "THE HURRICANE" KANE, captain and **ENGLAND**'s all-time top goal scorer, and **JUDE BELLINGHAM**, all-around amazing midfielder

UEFA Players to Watch

NETHERLANDS

VIRGIL VAN DIJK is one of the best defenders of his generation.

CROATIA

CROATIA's **LUKA MODRIĆ** continues to shine as one of the best midfielders of all time.

NORWAY

NORWAY's speedy striker **ERLING HAALAND** is one of the best players in the world.

BELGIUM

KEVIN DE BRUYNE, a midfielder known for his exceptional passing, playmaking, and goal scoring.

SWEDEN

Exceptional striker **ALEXANDER ISAK**.

ITALY

JORGINHO, a defensive midfielder who's won major titles for club and country.

CONMEBOL

THE SOUTH AMERICAN FOOTBALL CONFEDERATION (Confederación Sudamericana de Fútbol) has ten member nations—and six direct spots in the 2026 World Cup. The seventh-place team gets to compete in the Inter-Confederation playoffs.

The CONMEBOL qualifiers are widely considered the *toughest* in the world. Why? Top teams, harsh climates, and a round-robin system where every team plays against every other team.

ARGENTINA

BOLIVIA

BRAZIL

CHILE

COLOMBIA

ECUADOR

PARAGUAY

PERU

URUGUAY

VENEZUELA

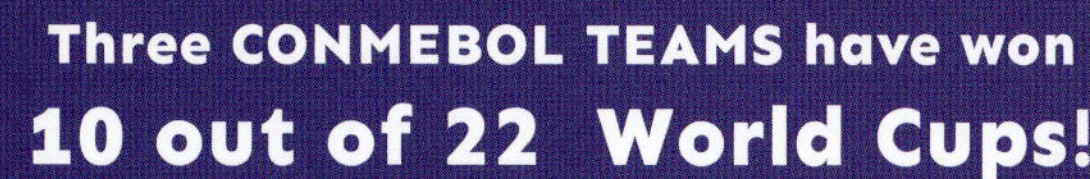

URUGUAY
1930, 1950

ARGENTINA
1978, 1986,
2022

BRAZIL
1958, 1962, 1970,
1994, and
2002

RECORD-HOLDER!
MOST WORLD CUP WINS
BY A SINGLE TEAM EVER!

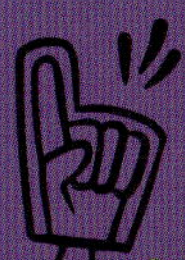

CONMEBOL

Hall of Fame

The 1970 tournament had the highest goals-per-game ratio of any World Cup ever!

SHOUT-OUT TO THE GREATEST SOCCER TEAM EVER:

BRAZIL'S 1970 NATIONAL TEAM!

Full of top-tier talent such as **Carlos Alberto**, **Pelé**, **Gérson**, **Jairzinho**, **Rivelino**, and **Tostão**, Brazil won EVERY SINGLE qualifying game in 1970 and all six games at the finals! It's the only time the winning team defeated the reigning European Champions, South American champions, *and* the World Cup's defending champions. *Wow!*

1970 was the first World Cup with substitutions!

Brazil was the champion in 2002 and made it all the way to the semifinals in 2014. Will 2026 be the year they reclaim the trophy?

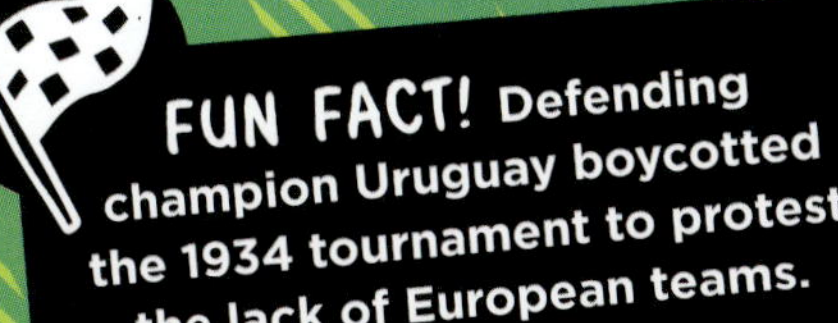

FUN FACT! Defending champion Uruguay boycotted the 1934 tournament to protest the lack of European teams.

URUGUAY

reached the quarterfinals in 2018 by defeating **Portugal** 2–1. Uruguayan striker **Edinson Cavani** scored twice—once on a header—to outshine **Portugal**'s **Cristiano Ronaldo**.

PERU

played in the 2018 World Cup for the first time since 1982. They beat **Australia** 2–0 in their group stage match with stellar goals by **André Carrillo** and **Paolo Guerrero**.

Peru's greatest player, **Teófilo Cubillas**, scored one of his two goals against **Morocco** in their 1970 group game.

Cubillas is Peru's Pelé! He scored a hat trick against Iran in the 1978 World Cup!

CONMEBOL Hall of Fame

CHILE defeated **Spain** in 2014 to make it to the Round of 16, where their game against **Brazil** went all the way to penalties!

FUN FACT! Chile hosted the 1962 World Cup after a major 1960 earthquake leveled half the country. The tournament went ahead, and Chile rose to third place—their best World Cup result ever—and beat top teams such as the USSR and Yugoslavia.

DISQUALIFIED! Chile refused to finish playing their 1989 qualifier against Brazil after their goalkeeper was hit by fireworks! Was he actually hit? *Nope!* Was the Chilean team allowed to play in the 1990 and 1994 World Cups? *Not a chance!*

Paraguay's star defender **Gustavo Gómez** takes on **Lionel Messi** in their 2026 World Cup qualifying game against **Argentina**.

PARAGUAY played in eight World Cups. Their best showing came in 2010 when they beat **Japan** 5–3 in the Round of 16 to advance to the quarterfinals against **Spain**.

BOLIVIA beat **Brazil** 2–0 in a qualifier to earn a spot in the 1994 World Cup—their first since 1950!

MAKING HISTORY! In 1998, **Paraguayan** goalkeeper **José Luis Chilavert** became the first goalie to take a direct free kick in a World Cup!

CONMEBOL

Memorable Moments

WHAT'S *THE* BIGGEST RIVALRY IN *ALL* OF SOCCER HISTORY?

BRAZIL V ARGENTINA

Brazil and Argentina have long been soccer's top two teams, with a player of the century— Pelé and Maradona— on each team. And both teams are favored to win in 2026. It's no wonder the competition between the countries is fierce!

GLORIOUS GOALS!

The top three goal scorers in the 2026 CONMEBOL World Cup qualifying matches are:

1. **Luis Díaz** (Colombia)
2. **Miguel Terceros** (Bolivia)
3. **Lionel Messi** (Argentina)

HOLY MOLY!
Argentina was accused of spiking a Brazilian player's water bottle with a sedative to make him sleepy before their 1990 group stage game in what became known as the the "Holy Water" game.

ARGENTINA'S
Diego Maradona made the 1986 World Cup legendary. He scored five goals and set up another five for his teammates— including the winning assist in the final against **Germany**. He created the foul of the century, the goal of the century, and the World Cup of the century!

1986 also saw an *epic* quarterfinal between Brazil and France that ended in a penalty shoot-out!

AWARD WINNER!

COLOMBIA'S

James Rodríguez controlled the ball with his chest, then turned and shot it past **Uruguay**'s goalkeeper from just beyond the penalty arc—with a goal so skillful, so beautiful, it won the Puskás Award for best goal of the year in 2014.

In **1990**, **COLOMBIAN** midfielder **Carlos Valderrama** cut through the **West German** defense with lightning quick passes and ultimately kicked the ball to **Freddy Rincón**, who scored an iconic goal!

James Rodríguez scored six goals in the 2014 World Cup and won the Golden Boot! He helped his team reach the quarterfinals—their highest standing yet!

2022 was the year **Lionel Messi** put the cap on a mind-blowing career. He scored seven goals in seven matches. Messi had finally won his World Cup.

Enner Valencia is **ECUADOR**'s top goal threat. He's scored a record six World Cup goals and the very first goal in the 2022 World Cup.

CONMEBOL

Players to Watch

Every CONMEBOL national team has its stars. Who will rise to the top in 2026?

COLOMBIA'S hopes ride on returning veteran and top goal scorers James Rodríguez and Luiz Diaz, who also play left winger and forward for Premier League team Liverpool.

ECUADOR'S 2026 national team has a talented roster of defensive players, including Willian Pacho, Perio Hincapié, and Joel Ordóñez. Can they best their team's 2006 rise into the Round of 16?

URUGUAY is looking for attackers like Frederico Valverde and Darwin Nuñez to bring back the magic.

But all eyes are on **ARGENTINA**. Can they do the impossible and win the World Cup two times in a row? With a roster full of superstars like midfielders Lionel Messi, Enzo Fernández, and Alexis Mac Allister and forwards Lautaro Martínez and Julian Alvarez, they just might!

BRAZIL has more World Cups than any other country and has raised some of the best players in the game—such as Pelé, Ronaldo, Ronaldinho, and Neymar. And for this World Cup, they're bringing back the star power. With returning legend Neymar, goalkeeper Alisson Becker, winger Raphinha, and forwards Endrick and Vinicius Junior, Brazil is one of the favorites to win in 2026.

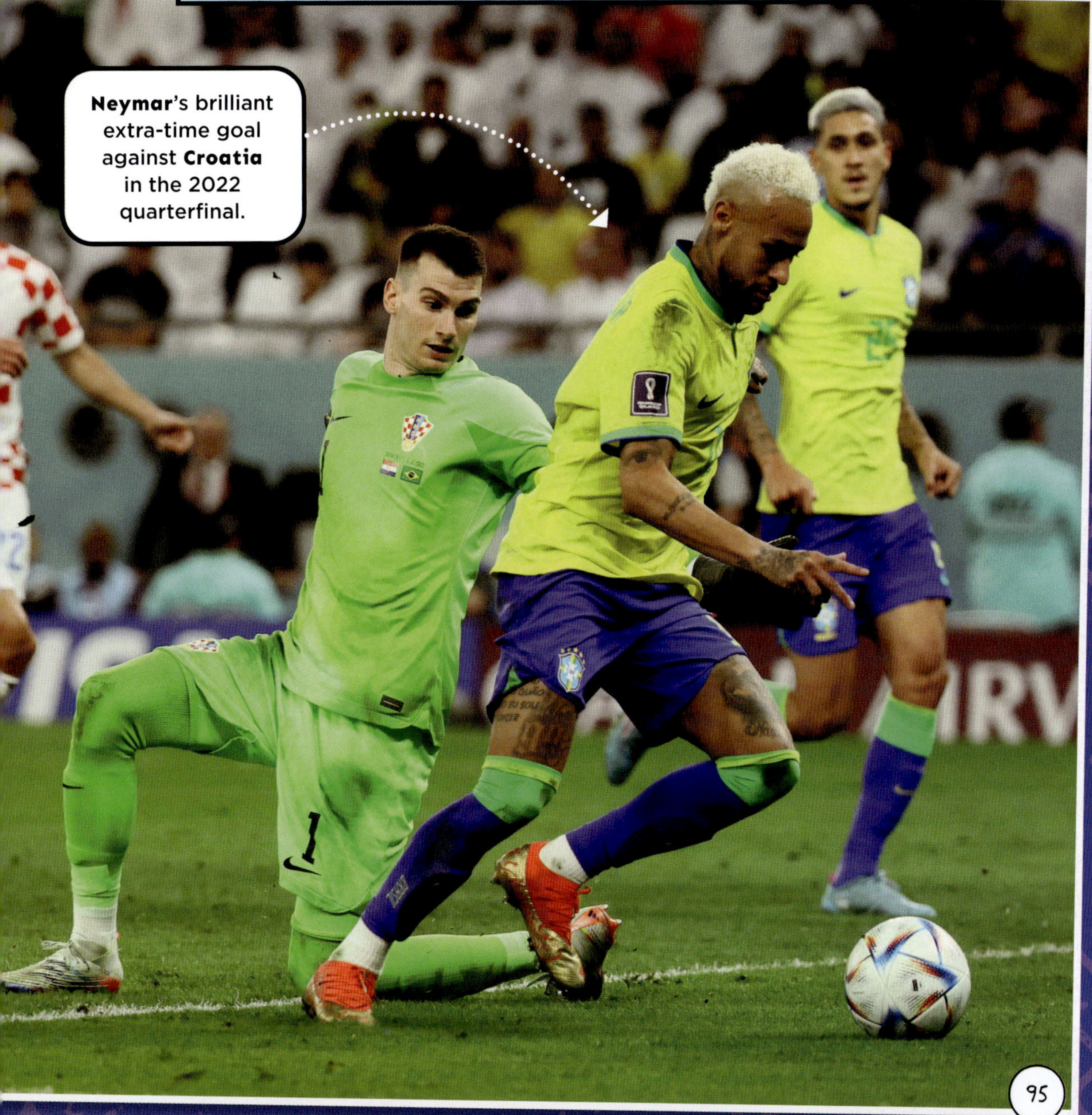

Neymar's brilliant extra-time goal against **Croatia** in the 2022 quarterfinal.

The Confederation of African Football

Nine African teams—out of fifty-four—are guaranteed spots in the 2026 World Cup. The top four runners-up will go head-to-head to see which one gets to play in the Inter-Confederation playoffs

ALGERIA

ANGOLA

BENIN

BOTSWANA

BURKINA FASO

BURUNDI

CAMEROON

CAPE VERDE

CENTRAL AFRICAN REPUBLIC

CHAD

COMOROS

CONGO

DJIBOUTI

DEMOCRATIC REPUBLIC OF THE CONGO

EGYPT

EQUATORIAL GUINEA

ERITREA

ESWATINI

ETHIOPIA

GABON

GAMBIA

GHANA

GUINEA

GUINEA-BISSAU

IVORY COAST

KENYA

LESOTHO

LIBERIA

LIBYA

MADAGASCAR

MALAWI

MALI
MAURITANIA
MAURITIUS
MOROCCO
MOZAMBIQUE
NAMIBIA
NIGER
NIGERIA
RWANDA
SÃO TOMÉ AND PRINCIPE
SENEGAL
SEYCHELLES
SIERRA LEONE
SOMALIA
SOUTH AFRICA
SOUTH SUDAN
SUDAN
TANZANIA
TOGO
TUNISIA
UGANDA
ZAMBIA
ZIMBABWE
TIME OUT FOR TRIVIA!
What was the first African and Arab nation to participate in the World Cup in 1934?
Answer: Egypt!
Mohamed Salah's stunning one-touch goal against **Saudi Arabia** in their 2018 group stage match. The **Egyptian** winger cut between two defenders and popped the ball right over the goalkeeper's head on his first touch—from the edge of the penalty box! Wow!
10
23
3
ALMOSAILEM
21

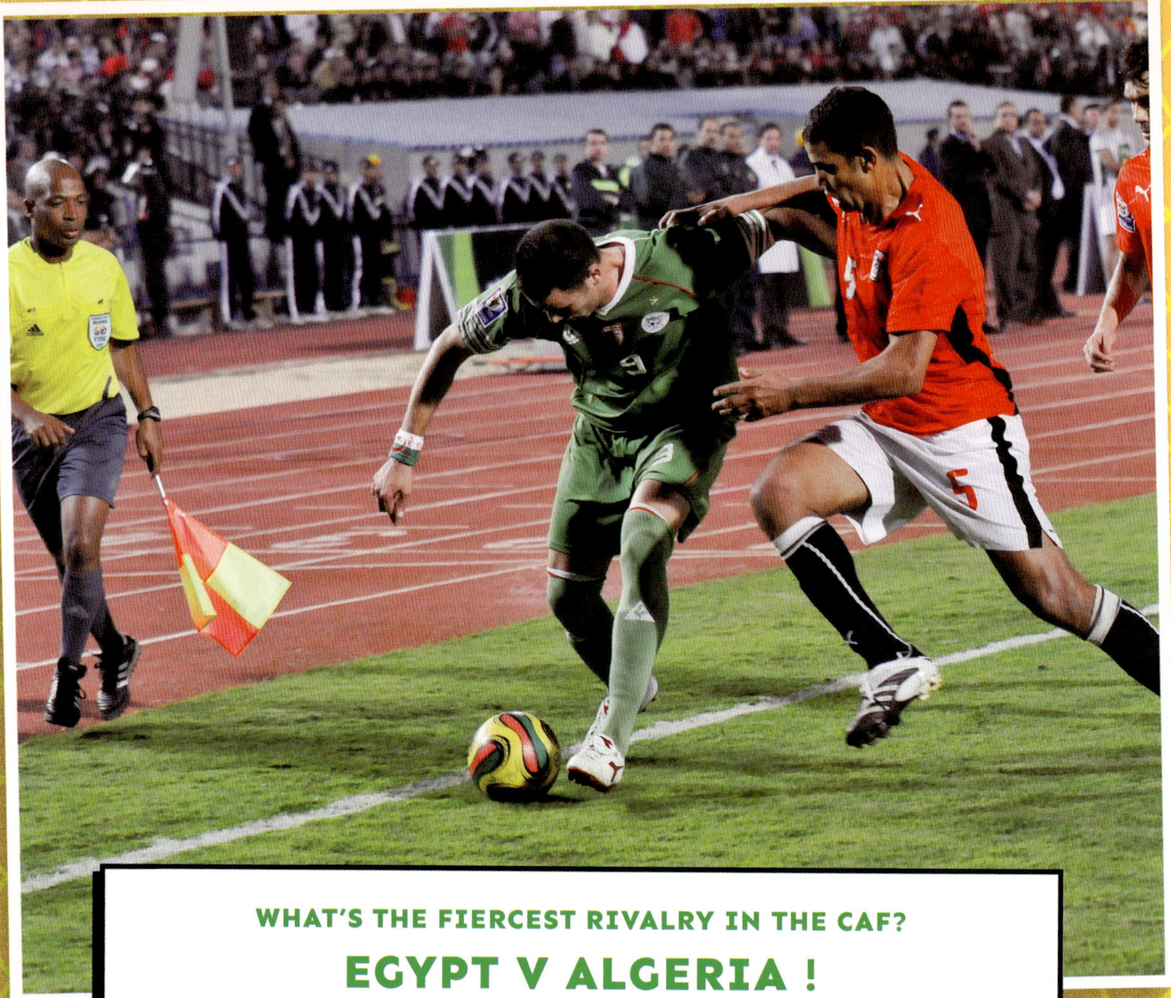

WHAT'S THE FIERCEST RIVALRY IN THE CAF?

EGYPT V ALGERIA !

Both Egypt and Algeria have passionate fans. In 1989, tensions flared when violence broke out after an aggressive World Cup qualifying game. And at a 2009 qualifier in Sudan, the tension was so high that 15,000 police officers were on hand to keep the peace!

RIVALRY OR COINCIDENCE?

GHANA faced the USA in group matches in the 2006, 2010, and 2014 World Cups—and the final score was 2–1 *every single time*! Ghana won in 2006 and 2010, and the USA won in 2014!

CAF

Hall of Fame

MOROCCO IS ONE OF THE HOSTS OF THE 2030 WORLD CUP!

2022 RECORD-BREAKER— MOROCCO!

Morocco beats Portugal 1–0 in the 2022 quarterfinals thanks to a header by Youssef En-Nesyri in the forty-second minute—and becomes the first African nation to make it to the semifinals.

Cristiano Ronaldo of **Portugal** vies with **Badr Benoun** and **Jawad El Yamiq** of **Morocco** during the quarterfinals of the 2022 World Cup.

CAF

Biggest Upsets!

In 1990, Cameroon becomes the first African nation to reach the quarterfinals by defeating powerhouse Argentina 1–0 in one of the biggest upsets in soccer history.

BERTIN EBWELLÉ of **CAMEROON** and **Óscar Ruggeri** of **Argentina** compete for the ball.

RECORD-BREAKER!

ROGER MILLA of **CAMEROON** scored 4 goals at the **1990 World Cup** at the age of 38—becoming the oldest goal scorer in World Cup history. Then he broke his own record in 1994 at 42 years old!

TUNISIA's victory against **MEXICO** in 1978 was the first time an African team had won a World Cup match.

SIPHIWE TSHABALALA celebrates after scoring an amazing goal for **SOUTH AFRICA** on home turf in their opening match against **MEXICO** in 2010.

PAPA BOUBA DIOP of **SENEGAL** pounces to score the opening goal against **FRANCE**.

THE "LIONS OF TERANGA," **SENEGAL,** beat defending champion **FRANCE** in the opening game of the 2002 World Cup—then go on to defeat **SWEDEN** in the Round of 16, making it all the way to the quarterfinals!

In 2014, Algerian forward **ISLAM SLIMANI** scores on a header to give **ALGERIA** a 1-1 draw with **RUSSIA**—and the team advances into the Round of 16 for the first time in history!

FUN FACT!
Liberian striker George Weah—who was voted African Player of the Century in 1996 and one of the best soccer players *never* to play at the World Cup—was elected President of Liberia in 2017.

TEAM TO WATCH

With a squad full of promising players, **ANGOLA** fought hard in their 2024–2025 World Cup qualifiers *and* qualified for the 2025 Africa Cup of Nations. How will they do in 2026?

ALGERIA has played in the 1982, 1986, 2010, and 2014 World Cups and made it to the Round of 16 in 2014!

The **NIGERIAN** "Super Eagles" played in six World Cups—and reached the Round of 16 in 1994.

TIME OUT FOR TRIVIA!

Who was the first sub-Saharan African team to play in the World Cup in 1974?

Answer: The Democratic Republic of the Congo (then known as Zaire).

IVORY COAST'S GOLDEN GENERATION

An extremely talented group of players—including **Didier Drogba** (*pictured here*), **Kolo** and **Yaya Touré**, and **Salomon Kalou**—all played their best at the same time (2005–2016) and led **Ivory Coast** to their first three World Cups (2006, 2010, 2014).

PLAYERS TO WATCH

There's a ton of top talent in the CAF, but in 2026, everyone is talking about **EGYPTIAN** captain and forward, **MOHAMED SALAH!**

Mohamed Salah is also a striker—and top scorer—for Premier League team Liverpool!

SADIO MANÉ is one of **SENEGAL**'s best wingers. He has also been playing for the Saudi Pro League club Al-Nassr since 2023!

WHO would YOU add to the list?

- Moroccan defender **ACHRAF HAKIMI?**
- Senegalese defender **KALIDOU KOULIBALY?**
- Egyptian midfielder **MOHAMED ELNENY?**
- Or Moroccan attacking midfielder **HAKIM ZIYECH?**

AFC

The Asian Football Confederation

The Asian Football Confederation (AFC) has 47 member nations and is sending eight teams to the World Cup. They also sent one team to the Inter-Confederation playoffs. Which teams will make history in 2026?

 AFGHANISTAN

 AUSTRALIA

 BAHRAIN

 BANGLADESH

 BHUTAN

 BRUNEI

 CAMBODIA

 CHINA

 CHINESE TAIPEI

 GUAM

 HONG KONG

 INDIA

 INDONESIA

 IRAN

 IRAQ

 JAPAN

 JORDAN

 KUWAIT

 KYRGYZSTAN

 LAOS

LEBANON

MACAU

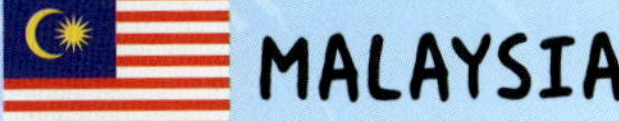
MALAYSIA

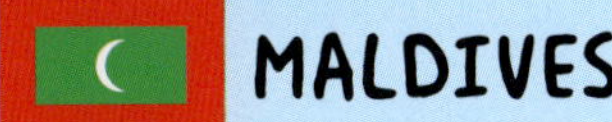
MALDIVES

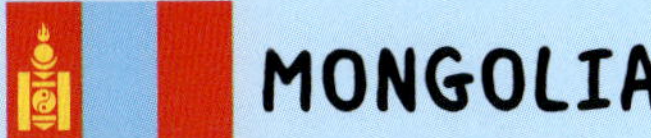
MONGOLIA

MYANMAR

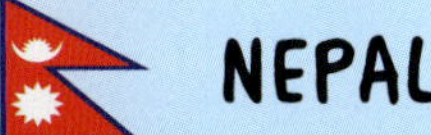
NEPAL

NORTH KOREA

NORTHERN MARIANA ISLANDS

OMAN

PAKISTAN

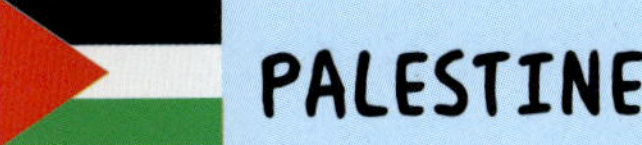
PALESTINE

PHILIPPINES

QATAR

SAUDI ARABIA

SINGAPORE

SOUTH KOREA

SRI LANKA

SYRIA

TAJIKISTAN

THAILAND

TIMOR-LESTE

TURKMENISTAN

UNITED ARAB EMIRATES

UZBEKISTAN

VIETNAM

YEMEN

TIME OUT FOR TRIVIA!

Which two AFC national teams were the first to qualify for the 2026 World Cup?

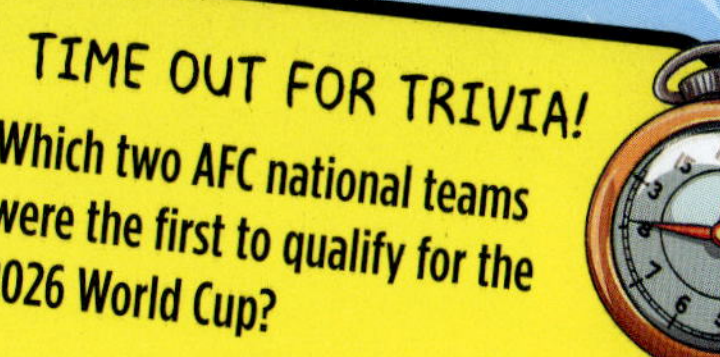

Answer: Japan and Iran qualified in March 2025.

WHAT'S THE BIGGEST RIVALRY IN THE AFC?

JAPAN V SOUTH KOREA!

Like many national soccer rivalries, it starts with politics. **Japan** and **Korea** started playing each other in 1954—only nine years after Japan's thirty-five-year occupation of South Korea ended in 1945. And their early matches got off to a rocky start when the South Korean president wouldn't even let Japan's players enter the country! Today, Japan and South Korea are on better terms. They hosted the tournament together in 2002 and have played in more World Cups than any other Arab or Asian nation. What will both teams achieve in 2026?

FUN FACT!
Japan and South Korea were the first Asian nations to host a World Cup!

JAPAN'S first World Cup win came during their second tournament in 2002 when **Junichi Inamoto** scored the winning goal against **Russia** in the fiftieth minute.

RECORD BREAKERS!

SOUTH KOREA became the first Asian team to reach the semifinals in 2002!

HISTORY MAKERS!

With a 2–1 score over **Colombia**, **Japan** became the first Asian nation that defeated a South American team in 2018.

AFC

World Cup Hall of Fame

2022: Japan's HIGH KEY Victory Against Spain in the Group Stage

In a dramatic game, Japan comes from behind to score two stunning goals early in the second half—by Kaoru Mitoma and Ritsu Doan. Japan ties with Spain, guaranteeing them a spot in the Round of 16 but leaving Spain to wait for the results of Germany's game with Costa Rica to see if they'd be heading home. Did Spain advance along with Japan? Yes, and the powerhouse German team were out of there!

2002: "Hiddink Magic" for South Korea

South Korea thrived on home soil for the 2002 World Cup. They beat Italy in the Round of 16 and Spain during a penalty shoot-out in the quarterfinals to step into the semis!

Some credit the new coach they'd hired a year and a half before the tournament—Guus Hiddink—but they also had an amazing squad with players like captain and defender Hong Myung-bo, midfielder Park Ji-sung, left-back Lee Young-pyo, and striker Ahn Jung-hwan!

NOTEWORTHY NICKNAMES

AUSTRALIA'S SOCCEROOS?

BHUTAN'S DRAGON BOYS?

OR THE MILLION ELEPHANTS OF LAOS?

Which AFC national team do YOU think has the best nickname?

AFC

World Cup Hall of Fame

IRAN has played in the World Cup six times, but their most memorable victory may be their first: a 1998 2–1 win over the **United States** that sent "the Yanks" packing. **Hamid Estili** and **Mehdi Mahdavikia** scored for **Iran**.

IRAQ played their first World Cup game—and scored their first World Cup goal—against **Belgium** in 1986.

AUSTRALIA has played in the World Cup six times. They made it all the way to the Round of 16 for the first time in 2006 by tying with **Croatia** on an amazing goal by winger **Harry Kewell** in the last ten minutes of the game.

MOROCCAN MIRACLE

Morocco's 2022 World Cup run was epic. With wins over top-ranked teams like **Belgium**, **Spain**, and **Portugal**. **Morocco** became the first African and Arab nation to make it to the semifinals!

ICONIC AFC GOALS!

1990: South Korean, Hwangbo Kwan's long-range goal against Spain in the group stage.

Instead of shooting a direct free kick, South Korean captain **Choi Soon-ho** tapped the ball to **Kwan Hwangbo**, who ran onto the ball, rocketing it into the top-right corner.

2014: Tim Cahill's Screamer v Netherlands in the group stage

Australia's **Tim Cahill** scored one of the best goals of the 2014 tournament with his left foot in the group stage. The ball looped over **Dutch** goalkeeper **Jasper Cillessen** and hit the crossbar on its way into the net!

2010: Keisuke Honda's 30-yard free kick against Denmark

Midfielder **Keisuke Honda**'s direct 30-yard free kick flew over the wall of the defensive players and into the Danish goal. **Japan** won 3–1 and advanced to the Round of 16. **Denmark** said "hej hej" ("bye-bye").

AFC

Top Takedowns in AFC History

DID SOMEBODY SAY, UPSET? SAUDI ARABIA turns around their group stage match against **ARGENTINA** in the second half with two goals scored in quick succession by **Saleh Al Shehri** and **Salem Al Dawsari**.

FUN FACT! The king of Saudi Arabia declared a public holiday to celebrate Saudi Arabia's win over Argentina!

JAPAN started off their 2022 tournament by beating four-time World Cup champion, **GERMANY**, 2–1 in the group stage! **Takuma Asano** scores his team's second goal.

NORTH KOREA became the first Asian team to reach the World Cup quarterfinals in 1966 by ousting **ITALY**!

PLAYERS TO WATCH

The AFC is full of top talent. Here are some players to look out for going into the 2026 tournament.

The "Miracle of Kazan" **SOUTH KOREA** sends **GERMANY** home from the 2018 World Cup in Kazan, Russia, with a shocking 2–0 defeat in their final group stage match.

Kim Young-gwon scores his country's first World Cup goal!

CHINA played in the 2022 World Cup. Can they do it again in 2026?

INDONESIA defeats **SAUDI ARABIA** and **BAHRAIN** (pictured here) during the 2026 World Cup qualifiers.

UZBEKISTAN hasn't made it to the World Cup before, but they have a top squad going into 2026 with players like **Abdukodir Khusanov**, **Abbosbek Fayzullaev**, and **Eldor Shomurodov**!

super striker MEHDI TAREMI of IRAN

He scored a second-half brace against **Uzbekistan** to secure a 2–2 draw and send his country to the 2026 World Cup.

JAPAN'S star forward TAKEFUSA KUBO

He scored **Japan's** second goal against **Bahrain** in the qualifier that guaranteed his country's spot in the 2026 World Cup.

SAUDI ARABIA'S veteran winger SALEM AL DAWSARI

Al Dawsari challenged **Ángel Di María** in **Saudi Arabia's** infamous 2022 win over **Argentina**.

SOUTH KOREAN captain SON HEUNG-MIN

He took a free kick during **South Korea's** 2026 qualifier against **Oman**.

OFC The Oceania Football Confederation

For the first time in World Cup history, one of the Oceania Football Confederation teams is guaranteed a spot in the World Cup. And the spot goes to . . . New Zealand!

AMERICAN SAMOA

COOK ISLANDS

FIJI

NEW CALEDONIA

NEW ZEALAND

PAPUA NEW GUINEA

SAMOA

SOLOMON ISLANDS

TAHITI

TONGA

VANUATU

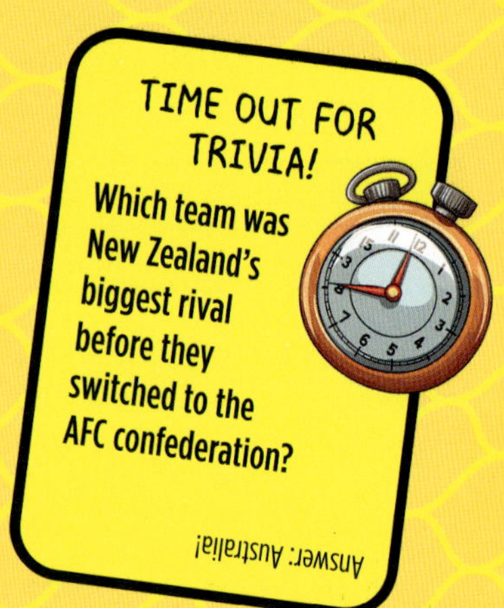

PLAYER TO WATCH: Captain, forward, and team top scorer for the New Zealand National Team, **Chris Wood**, during a friendly match between Republic of Ireland and New Zealand in 2023.

FUN FACT! The team nickname is the "All Whites" because of their uniforms. And the team's supporters are called the "White Noise"!

NEW CALEDONIA landed a spot in the Inter-Confederation playoff tournament for a chance to qualify for the World Cup for the *very first time*. How do you rate their chances?

World Cup Superstitions

ROUND TWO!

Superstitions give players, fans, and even coaches a feeling of control in a tournament where a lot is up to chance. Here are a few things they've done to bring on the good luck.

Former **Ivory Coast** center-back **Kolo Touré** (right) insisted on being the last player to step on the field. He even got a yellow card once during club play because he refused to take the field before an injured teammate.

1978
Argentine star striker **Mario Kempes** suffered a scoring slump until he shaved off his horseshoe mustache.

Former **Sierra Leone** midfielder **Malvin Kamara** watched the movie *Willy Wonka & the Chocolate Factory* before every game to chill out and feel lucky.

England's **Dele Alli** wore the same shin guards he'd worn since childhood throughout the 2018 World Cup.

Italy's **Daniele De Rossi** wore a shirt with a short right sleeve and a long left sleeve for every 2012 World Cup Game.

English defender **Phil Jones**—who retired in 2023—refused to step on any white lines.

England's 1966 World Cup-winning captain, **Bobby Moore,** *had* to be the last player to pull on his shorts.

At the 1994 World Cup, **USMT** defender **Alexei Lalas** warmed up before every game in a gray Hamilton College T-shirt. He thought it would bring him good luck because his dad went there!

French legend **Thierry Henry**—who is now a coach and commentator—always put his left sock on before his right to keep his confidence high on the field.

Former **English** striker **Gary Lineker**—who retired in 1994—refused to take any shots on goal during warm-ups. He was saving his goals for the game!

Former **German** soccer player **Mesut Özil,** who retired in 2023, always tied his laces with multiple knots and *always* put on his right cleat first.

Colombia's 1990 World Cup goalkeeper **René Higuita** only wore blue underwear to games.

COACHES CORNER

Argentina's 1986 coach Carlos Bilardo wouldn't let his players eat chicken because he believed it brought bad luck.

Luiz Felipe Scolari, the Brazilian coach who led his team to victory in 2002, brought a protective amulet to games. Did it work? His team won the tournament!

Moroccan coach Hervé Renard wore a white shirt to every game of the 2022 World Cup in Russia. Why? Because he was wearing a white shirt when his team won a surprise victory against Zambia at the Africa Cup of Nations in 2012. Did it work? Nope! Morocco was sent packing after the group stage.

Top Five Shadiest World Cup Moments

With almost one hundred years of history, some wild things are bound to happen in the World Cup. And these top six are downright sus.

1.

DEVIOUS DICTATOR, 1934

Italian dictator **Benito Mussolini** "greased palms" to host the 1934 World Cup. Italy then used bribery and intimidation to make it easier for Italy to win first place.

2.

PRINCELY PROTEST! 1982

The score was 4–0 in favor of France at Kuwait's 1982 World Cup debut when **the prince of Kuwait** blew a whistle, stepped onto the field, and got the referee to overturn France's fourth goal! Kuwait still lost, and the ref was banned from all future games!

3.

CONTROVERSIAL COLLISION, 1982

West German goalkeeper **Harald Schumacher** brutally collided in the air with **French** defender **Patrick Battison** during the semifinal match between West Germany and France. He knocked out Battison *and* Battison's front teeth along with cracking three of his ribs.

ROBBED WITHOUT A RED! Did the goalie get a red card? *No!* He played on and West Germany won the game in a penalty shoot-out (the first World Cup game ever decided by a penalty shoot-out!).

THE IMMORTAL NUMBER 2, 1994

Star **Colombian** defender **Andrés Escobar** is killed in his hometown one month after he accidentally scored an own-goal in a group stage match against the US that led to Colombia's elimination from the 1994 World Cup.

5.

THE DISGRACE OF GIJÓN, 1982

Germany and **Austria** agreed to end their group stage match with a score of 1–0 in favor of Germany so they'd both advance to the finals. Their "gentlemen's agreement" got them booed off the field, sent top-tier team Algeria packing, and changed the rules of soccer forever.

GAME CHANGER! In 1966, Argentina's Antonio Rattín insulted the queen and messed with the UK flag after claiming the refs were favoring England. English fans threw chocolate at him in protest. It's one reason red cards were invented!

Famous Fans

Which celebrities will be watching the 2026 World Cup?

Is Jenna Ortega a Messi fan? She says she admires him and has been spotted at his Inter Miami MLS (Major League Soccer) games.

Tom Holland is a fan of British club team Tottenham Hotspur. Did Zendaya become a Spurs fan for Tom Holland or has she always loved soccer?

Who else is a Tottenham Spurs fan? English pop singer and songwriter **Adele**.

Singer, songwriter, and actor **Olivia Rodrigo** was spotted at a Manchester United v Chelsea game at a Premier League soccer game.

Singer-songwriter **Ed Sheeran** had a front-row seat when England beat the Netherlands in the Euro Cup 2024 final.

Actors **Ryan Reynolds** and **Rob McElhenney** love soccer so much they bought a Welsh team: Wrexham AFC!

Actor **Margot Robbie** supports her team—Fulham FC!

Justin Bieber likes to watch—and play!—soccer.

LeBron James with **Serena Williams** and **Kim Kardashian** watch Messi play in Miami.

Cheering Section!

It's no secret that sports teams play their best when they have a stadium full of fans cheering them on. From homemade signs to the wave to noise-makers like the vuvuzelas blown in the 2010 World Cup in South Africa, fans know how to make their support—and disappointments—known!

DID YOU KNOW?

The wave started in **MEXICO**! "The Mexican Wave" or "La Ola" became a global phenomenon after Mexican fans showed off the move at the 1986 World Cup in Mexico.

RECORD-BREAKING CROWDS!

A record-breaking **5.5 million fans** are expected to watch the 2026 World Cup matches in person at stadiums across the US, Mexico, and Canada. Six *billion viewers* will tune in around the world!

THE AMERICAN OUTLAWS

are a group of soccer fans who support the US Men's and Women's national teams and travel around the world to cheer them on.

FUN FACT! Canadian soccer fans are known as "The Canucks" or "Les Rouges" (The Reds)!

PHOTO CREDITS:

Page iii Adobe Stock: Sampao - stock.adobe.com
Page vi Alamy: Andre Paes / Alamy Stock Photo
Page 1 Adobe Stock: HeGraDe – stock.adobe.com
Page 3 Adobe Stock: Nikolay N. Antonov - stock.adobe.com
Page 6 Alamy: Dom Slike / Alamy Stock Photo, ZUMA Press, Inc. / Alamy Stock Photo
Page 7 Alamy: NurPhoto SRL / Alamy Stock Photo
Page 10 Alamy: PA Images / Alamy Stock Photo
Page 14 Alamy: Action Plus Sports Images / Alamy Stock Photo
Page 16 Alamy: Sportimage Ltd / Alamy Stock Photo
Page 17 Alamy: Independent Photo Agency / Alamy Stock Photo
Page 18 Alamy: DPPI Media / Alamy Stock Photo, Daniel Motz / Alamy Stock Photo
Page 19 Alamy: Xinhua / Alamy Stock Photo, dpa picture alliance / Alamy Stock Photo
Page 20 Alamy: PA Images / Alamy Stock Photo
Page 21 Adobe Stock: Adi - stock.adobe.com, master1305 – stock.adobe.com
Page 22 Alamy: Sportimage Ltd / Alamy Stock Photo
Page 24 Alamy: Sportimage Ltd / Alamy Stock Photo
Page 25 Alamy: Xinhua / Alamy Stock Photo
Page 26 Alamy: ANP / Alamy Stock Photo
Page 27 Alamy: SOPA Images Limited / Alamy Stock Photo
Page 28 Shutterstock: catwalker / Shutterstock.com
Page 29 Alamy: dpa picture alliance / Alamy Stock Photo, Aflo Co. Ltd. / Alamy Stock Photo
Page 30 Alamy: SOPA Images Limited / Alamy Stock Photo
Page 31 Alamy: ZUMA Press, Inc. / Alamy Stock Photo, NurPhoto SRL / Alamy Stock Photo
Page 32 Alamy: BNA Photographic / Alamy Stock Photo, dpa picture alliance / Alamy Stock Photo
Page 33 Alamy: Kolvenbach / Alamy Stock Photo, dpa picture alliance / Alamy Stock Photo
Page 34 Alamy: PA Images / Alamy Stock Photo, Pa Images / Alamy Stock Photo
Page 35 Shutterstock: Andre Teixeira / Shutterstock.com
Page 36 Alamy: ZUMA Press Inc / Alamy Stock Photo
Page 37 Alamy: Abaca Press / Alamy Stock Photo
Page 41 Alamy: Smith Archive / Alamy Stock Photo
Page 42 Alamy: PA Images / Alamy Stock Photo
Page 43 Alamy: Sportimage Ltd / Alamy Stock Photo, Zume Press Inc. / Alamy Stock Photo
Page 44 Alamy: Aflo Co. Ltd. / Alamy Stock Photo, PA Images / Alamy Stock Photo
Page 45 Alamy: PA Images / Alamy Stock Photo
Page 46 Alamy: Sportimage Ltd / Alamy Stock Photo, dpa picture alliance / Alamy Stock Photo, PA Images / Alamy Stock Photo
Page 47 Alamy: Xinhua / Alamy Stock Photo
Page 48 Alamy: dpa picture alliance / Alamy Stock Photo
Page 49 Alamy: Allstar Picture Library Ltd / Alamy Stock Photo, PA Images / Alamy Stock Photo
Page 50 Alamy: Action Plus Sports Images / Alamy Stock Photo
Page 56 Shutterstock: Poetra.RH / Shutterstock.com
Page 57 Shutterstock: Cosmin Iftode / Shutterstock.com
Page 58 Shutterstock: Ringo Chiu / Shutterstock.com, Alamy: Xinhua / Alamy Stock Photo
Page 60 Alamy: PA Images / Alamy Stock Photo
Page 62 Alamy: Zuma Press, Inc. / Alamy Stock Photo
Page 63 Alamy: Allstar Picture Library Ltd / Alamy Stock Photo, Allstar Picture Library Ltd / Alamy Stock Photo
Page 66 Alamy: PA Images / Alamy Stock Photo
Page 67 Alamy: Image of sport / Alamy Stock Photo
Page 68 Alamy: Sipa USA / Alamy Stock Photo
Page 69 Alamy: Eyepix Group / Alamy Stock Photo, PA Images / Alamy Stock Photo
Page 70 Shutterstock: oasisamuel / Shutterstock.com
Page 71 Shutterstock: Ringo Chiu / Shutterstock.com
Page 72 Alamy: PA Images / Alamy Stock Photo
Page 73 Shutterstock: Marco Iacobucci Epp / Shutterstock.com
Page 76 Shutterstock: Dokshin Vlad / Shutterstock.com
Page 77 Alamy: UPI / Alamy Stock Photo
Page 78 Shutterstock: katatonia82 / Shutterstock.com
Page 79 Alamy: PA Images
Page 80 Shutterstock: Celso Pupo / Shutterstock.com, Gevorg Ghazaryan / Shutterstock.com
Page 82 Shutterstock: Vitalii Vitleo / Shutterstock.com, Maciej Rogowski Photo / Shutterstock.com
Page 83 Shutterstock: Mikolaj Barbanell / Shutterstock.com, ph.FAB / Shutterstock.com
Page 84 Shutterstock: Orange Pictures / Shutterstock.com, Victor Velter / Shutterstock.com
Page 85 Shutterstock: ph.FAB / Shutterstock.com, Thomas Persson / Shutterstock.com
Page 88 Alamy: Historic Collection / Alamy Stock Photo
Page 89 Alamy: Zeytun Sports Images / Alamy Stock Photo
Page 90 Alamy: PRESSINPHOTO SPORTS AGENCY / Alamy Stock Photo, Shutterstock: Celso Pulpo / Shutterstock.com
Page 91 Alamy: DiaEsportivo / Alamy Stock Photo
Page 92 Alamy: PA Images / Alamy Stock Photo
Page 93 Alamy: INTERFOTO / Alamy Stock Photo, Shutterstock: Celso Pupo / Shutterstock.com
Page 94 Alamy: Néstor J. Beremblum / Alamy Stock Photo
Page 95 Alamy: Xinhua / Alamy Stock Photo
Page 97 Alamy: dpa picture alliance / Alamy Stock Photo
Page 98 Alamy: Claudia Wiens / Alamy Stock Photo
Page 99 Alamy: SPP Sport Press Photo. / Alamy Stock Photo
Page 100 Alamy: INTERFOTO / Alamy Stock Photo, PA Images / Alamy Stock Photo
Page 101 Alamy: dpa picture alliance / Alamy Stock Photo, PA Images / Alamy Stock Photo, Xinhua / Alamy Stock Photo
Page 102 Alamy: Cal Sport Media / Alamy Stock Photo, Aflo Co. Ltd. / Alamy Stock Photo
Page 103 Alamy: Xinhua / Alamy Stock Photo, Shutterstock: A.RICARDO / Shutterstock.com
Page 106 Alamy: UPI / Alamy Stock Photo
Page 107 Alamy: Abaca Press / Alamy Stock Photo
Page 108 Alamy: tony quinn / Alamy Stock Photo, Kolvenbach / Alamy Stock Photo
Page 109 Alamy: MB Media Solutions / Alamy Stock Photo, Shutterstock: feelphoto / Alamy Stock Photo
Page 110 Alamy: SPP Sport Press Photo. / Alamy Stock Photo, PA Images / Alamy Stock Photo, dpa picture alliance / Alamy Stock Photo
Page 111 Alamy: Xinhua / Alamy Stock Photo
Page 113 Alamy: Sipa USA / Alamy Stock Photo
Page 114 Alamy: Abaca Press / Alamy Stock Photo, Fabio Diena / Alamy Stock Photo
Page 115 Alamy: Xinhua / Alamy Stock Photo, Shutterstock: ph.Fab / Shutterstock.com
Page 116 Alamy: MGPhoto76 / Alamy Stock Photo
Page 117 Alamy: PA Images / Alamy Stock Photo, dpa picture alliance / Alamy Stock Photo
Page 118 Alamy: Jeffrey Mayer / Alamy Stock Photo
Page 119 Alamy: WENN Rights Ltd / Alamy Stock Photo, Getty Images: Icon Sportswire via Getty Images
Page 120 Alamy: Daniel Ernst / Alamy Stock Photo, A.PAES / Alamy Stock Photo, Informa Plus Photo Agency / Alamy Stock Photo
Page 121 Alamy: Fauzan Fitria / Alamy Stock Photo

WHAT'S UP NEXT?

Fans will flock to **Spain**, **Portugal**, and **Morocco** for the 2030 World Cup!

100th ANNIVERSARY!

The first three games of the 2030 World Cup will take place in Paraguay, Uruguay, and Argentina to celebrate the centenary in the birthplace of the World Cup, South America!

TIME OUT FOR TRIVIA!

Which World Cup game hosted the most fans for any soccer game ever?

Answer: The 1950 final between Uruguay and Brazil! 173,850 tickets were sold but more than 200,000 fans actually showed up for the game!

AND AFTER THAT?

See you in Saudi Arabia in 2034!